The *LMS &* *LNER* *in*
Manchester

The *LMS* & *LNER* in Manchester

R. E. Rose

LONDON
IAN ALLAN LTD

Contents

First published 1987

ISBN 0 7110 1708 5

Published by Ian Allan Ltd, Shepperton, Surrey;
and printed by Ian Allan Printing Ltd at their works
at Coombelands in Runnymede, England

Introduction

In 1923, at the time of Grouping, Manchester had
five main line stations if one included Mayfield.
Mayfield, built in 1910, was adjacent to and served
as an overflow for the LNWR terminus at London
Road. The Great Central (GC) side of London Road
and the Cheshire Lines Committee (CLC) station,
Central, were also termini. The Manchester South
Junction and Altrincham suburban line also had
stations in the city at London Road and Oxford
Road. Indeed, the latter had at one time been the
terminus and was destined to take up that role again
in British Railways days. The Lancashire &
Yorkshire (L&Y), also had a busy four-platform
station at Salford about 44 chains east of their
Victoria station. One-time passenger termini at
Liverpool Road and Oldham Road were still in use
as goods depots.

Within easy reach of the city were six large engine
sheds, the LMS being represented by Longsight
(LNWR) which had 12 through-roads with access at
either end. Patricroft (LNWR) consisted of two
buildings, both dead-end, one facing south the
other east. Newton Heath (L&Y) sported 24
through-roads extending about three chains either
side of the building but ending against a wall at the
rear, and Agecroft (L&Y) seven dead-end roads.
The LNER was at Gorton (GC) shed which featured
24 dead-end roads, four of which were rather
shorter than the remainder. Alongside were the
extensive locomotive works buildings, and just
across the main line were those of Beyer Peacock.
The CLC were at Trafford Park, with 20 dead-end
roads which housed locomotives of both LMS and
LNER. Large and spacious, Trafford Park had
replaced cramped accommodation at Cornbrook
during the 1890s. The LMS also inherited a small
Midland roundhouse at Belle Vue, situated between
the Great Central main line and the Great Central &
Midland Joint line to Marple. By the 1930s its status
was reduced to the stabling of goods engines only,

but it had housed the odd passenger engine earlier, and, earlier still, tank engines for working a long-forgotten local service. Six miles away at Stockport Edgeley was a busy (LNWR) shed and the CLC had a shed at Heaton Mersey, a short distance from the Stockport Tiviot Dale station. Here, as at Trafford Park, engines from both the LMS and LNER were stabled. Within easy reach of Manchester were L&Y sheds at Bolton, Bury and Oldham (Lees) and the L&Y works at Horwich. The LNWR was also represented at Bolton (Plodder Lane). Mention should perhaps be made of a tiny Great Northern (GN) shed situated at that company's Deansgate goods yard. Intended no doubt to house the 'J52' tank engines which shunted the yard there seems every probability the shed was never used; certainly it was not used in LNER days.

A striking feature of the scene was the number of substantial viaducts in and around the city. Travel into Manchester on any route and one would be travelling over a viaduct. Perhaps the *pièce-de-résistance* in this field is the superb brick viaduct over the River Mersey at Stockport. About one-third of a mile long, it towers over 100ft above the river, and consists of 27 arches. Originally there had only been 26. It is said that 11 million bricks were used in its construction. The original double-track viaduct was completed in under two years in December 1840; in 1889 it was widened to accommodate four tracks.

On reflection, it seems likely that nowhere outside London could a more varied panorama of locomotives, rolling stock and general railwayana have been found. During the period between the wars the services were increasing, in particular the local services to the gradual outward spread of the population. There was a steady increase in the number of day and half-day excursion trains provided, especially at weekends. Engines from a great many sheds were daily visitors, including a handful of Great Western engines working through from Chester to Manchester Exchange. The volume of traffic made it inevitable that the odd failure en route would occur resulting in ever greater variety. An added attraction was the Manchester Ship Canal Railway which had about 70 tank engines of several varieties in stock at any one time, which also provided the motive power for the 33 miles of the Trafford Park Estates Railway.

Naturally, the high density of traffic combined with human fallibility resulted in the occasional mishap — nothing, however, of sufficient gravity to detract from the then widely held opinion that the railways of Great Britain afforded the safest means of transport in the world.

In the following pages I shall endeavour to portray the scene as I saw it. Obviously it is impossible to cover every aspect in one volume, but I hope to give younger readers some insight into the scene which I knew and loved for so many years. For older readers I can perhaps evoke a few pleasant if nostalgic memories.

Acknowledgements

My grateful thanks are due, especially to Dorothy Margerison, widow of my dear friend Hubert Margerison, for the use of her late husband's notebooks and diaries; also to the staff of the Library of Social Services and the Local History Library in Manchester; to Alan Brown, David Jackson, S. D. Johnson, Eric Neve and Owen Russell who have assisted with items of which they had special knowledge; and finally, to Peter Helm, Chris Heaps and again Alan Brown for considerable assistance with the period from 1939 onwards.

Davyhulme, Manchester
1987   *Eric Rose*

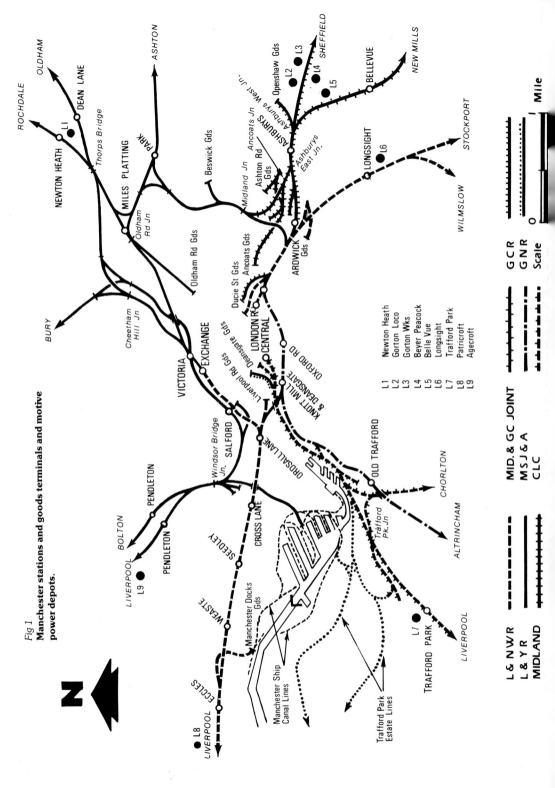

Fig 1
Manchester stations and goods terminals and motive power depots.

L1 Newton Heath
L2 Gorton Loco
L3 Gorton Wks
L4 Beyer Peacock
L5 Belle Vue
L6 Longsight
L7 Trafford Park
L8 Patricroft
L9 Agecroft

L&NWR
L&YR
MIDLAND
MID.&GC JOINT
MSJ&A
CLC
GCR
GNR

Scale

0   Mile

6

1 London Road

LMS

First opened over 80 years before Grouping, enlarged and improved during the intervening years, the London Road terminus of the LNWR would have been considered by many enthusiasts and intending passengers to be Manchester's 'Main' station. It is likely that most London passengers would select the North-West route, offering as it did the quickest and slightly shorter route, with a journey time of 3hr 30min. From its side of the station the LNER had a best time to Marylebone of 4hr 23min and to King's Cross of 5hr 29min. Across town at Central one could board a Midland train for St Pancras, the shortest journey time to which was 4hr.

Platform 1 and Platforms 3 to 7 at London Road (strangely there was not a Platform 2) were those of the LMS. These were open platforms — tickets being collected at either Stockport or Longsight. As one entered the station the three platforms to the extreme left were the property of the LNER, having previously belonged to the Manchester, Sheffield &

Lincoln Railway (MS&L) and GC. To avoid any confusion these platforms were designated A, B and C. A small point which always caught my attention was the description of local trains on the indicator boards. On the LMS side the legend read, for example, 'All stations to Stockport, the LNER, Glossop and all intermediate stations'.

There was an unfortunate bottle-neck at the outlet from the LMS platforms which proved increasingly difficult as train travel became ever more popular as the years went by. By the mid-1930s the down 'Lancastrian' in particular became such a problem on Friday and Saturday evenings, loads of 16 bogies being commonplace, that the last six coaches were dropped at Wilmslow and worked down a few minutes later by a Stockport tank engine. Enthusiasts were thus treated to the sight of an unsuperheated 'Precursor' tank charging down the bank from Gatley to East Didsbury sporting express headlamps. The acceptance of 16 coaches into Platform 4, the main arrival

Right:
Early 1930s view from footbridge at London Road. A 'George The Fifth' backs into Platform 1. A LNWR tender engine and a Coal Tank are in the turntable area. In the distance a GC tank engine proceeds towards Ardwick with empty stock. Another tank engine is just visible beyond the 'George'. *W. Potter*

Right:
**LMS-built 'Compound' No 1111
in old style livery alongside
Longsight shed. Date unknown.**
W. Potter

Below:
**Another LMS-built 'Compound'
No 1110 in the later style livery,
is seen near Heaton Chapel with
a West of England train, in about
1938.** *W. Potter*

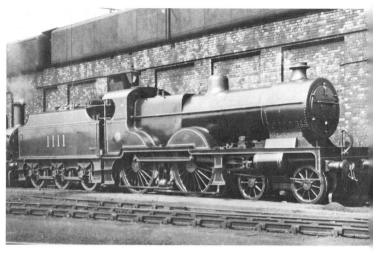

Above:
**LNWR 'Watford' 0-6-2T No 6912 looking very smart at
Longsight in July 1937. With No 6900, 6912 survived
into BR days.** *W. Potter*

platform for London trains, would have blocked the access to Platforms 5 to 7.

The most popular vantage point for the young spotter was the far end of Platform 3 which gave a grandstand view of both sides of the main station and an uninterrupted view of the three platforms of the Manchester South Junction & Altrincham (MSJ&A) line immediately to the south. This latter was the terminus of the MSJ&A, the tracks along Platforms 1 and 2 connecting with the main line. The occasional pick-up goods or passenger excursion train might pass through. Every hour or so a passenger train would arrive or depart off the Lymm line which joined the MSJ&A at Timperley and served Warrington Low Level, Widnes and Liverpool Lime Street. A footbridge ran over the platforms connecting the three sections and crossed over the adjacent Fairfield Street to link up with Mayfield. At the point where the steps led down to Platform 1 the LNER had a barrier and booth which housed the ticket inspector.

During the 1920s my own visits to London Road were brief and infrequent and it is true to say that my strongest memories are of incidents which merited mention in the local press. Thanks to the most excellent library facilities in Manchester I have been able, in most cases, to refresh my memory and check dates and details. With a few exceptions my own notes on locomotives do not predate 1930; although I had been an avid observer of the railway scene, wherever and whenever the opportunity arose, since about 1924. It was not until about 1930 that I began to take notes seriously.

On the LMS side it would seem likely that there were no great changes in the period immediately after grouping — indeed I would expect the same was the case everywhere. For instance, it is known that 'Jumbos' and 'Renowns' could still be found working, albeit not on the best jobs except perhaps as a pilot. They had largely disappeared by 1930

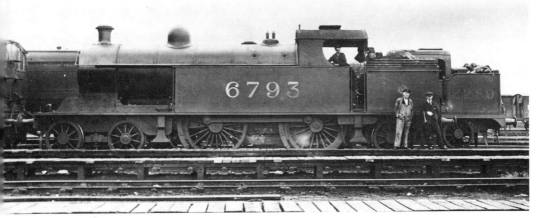

but the other LNWR passenger engines still had a little time left. The 'Claughton' engines which were fitted with the larger boiler were soon on the scene, one of which came to grief on an express as I will describe later. When the Midland 'Compounds' were first multiplied they were tried on most of the express services, indeed Longsight had eight on strength throughout the 1930s but they were largely confined to use on secondary express turns. Local services were largely in charge of tank engines and of course LNWR types held sway until the advent of Fowler's most excellent 2-6-4T; indeed they still continued to have a large share of the traffic until the Stanier tanks began to appear a dozen or so years later. Rather strangely perhaps, three of the ex-Midland 0-4-4T engines arrived at Longsight in the early 1930s, one of which might usually be found working between Mayfield and Wilmslow via the Styal line in the centre of four coaches. If my memory serves me well the two coaches ahead of the engine were dispensed with on a Sunday. The well provided Buxton commuter services were the special province of Fowler's 2-6-4 'Prince' tanks once they had become established, although in about 1929 the Hughes Baltic tanks were given a trial on this line. Other regular tank engine visitors were the various types of North Staffs engines working the Macclesfield & Stoke-on-Trent line. These very neat and attractive engines invariably gave a good account of themselves; the 0-6-4 variety frequently appearing on fast trains in early days. They were the most modern tank engines inherited by the LMS, and I would suggest that only their small number prevented them from enjoying

longer lives. The five 4-4-0s of North Stafford origin would also have been regular visitors I imagine, although I only recall noting one on one occasion. The LMS originally numbered these engines with the Midland series but when further Class 2P 4-4-0s were built the North Staffs engines were renumbered after the 'George the Fifth' engines. Longsight had two or so LNWR 'Watford' 0-6-2T engines, one of which (No 6912) remained well into the 1930s by which time it was confined largely to station pilot and empty stock working. I recall that in about 1934 she returned from a works visit rather well turned out with transfer figures and letters; she must have been one of the last LNWR tank engines to be so favoured, unlined black and plain yellow figures becoming the order of the day.

By the early 1930s one would have noticed that the times of many trains had improved; for instance the best time to London had been reduced to 3hr 15min. Restaurant and sleeping car facilities were also improving. The through train between Manchester and Bournemouth had been named the 'Pines Express' and the working to certain South Coast resorts the 'Sunny South Express'. A morning visit to London Road during this period would find numerous tank engines of the types mentioned still in evidence, along with one or two 'Jinty' 0-6-0Ts in the goods yard or perhaps on empty stock workings. As the years went by one would notice these little stalwarts returning from visits to the works with their 16xxx series numbers replaced by 7xxx series. Likewise the Hughes 2-6-0s and, when they arrived on the scene, the Stanier 2-6-0s would also be renumbered from the 13000-13284 series to 2700-2984. For what it may be worth I will mention that in those days the 40 Stanier engines were classified '4F' although the Hughes engines were always '5P/4F'. I cannot offer an opinion on the merits of the Stanier engines; they were always rather rare in Manchester during my time. The only

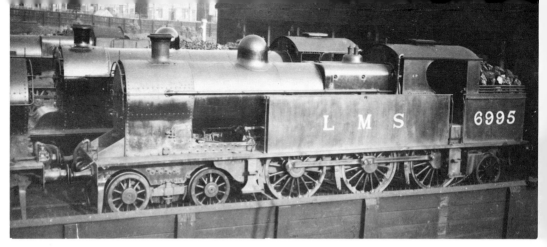

Above:

'Prince' Tank No 6995 in later style livery June 1935. Edgeley shed in background after completion of new roof. *W. Potter*

occasion on which I can recall any of them stationed in the area was during a short period in about 1934 when Nos 13260 and 2961 were at Longsight. I once saw the latter on station pilot duty but the only other occasions on which I saw either they were on shed. Longsight had Nos 2856 and 2858 for a long time, but I do not recall them being employed very much other than on fitted goods turns and possibly the odd stopping train to Crewe. This is really rather strange as I found them exceedingly popular among footplatemen every-where else on the system. Stockport had Nos 2775 and 2776 throughout the 1930s. This pair was among the last I saw in red livery with the five-figure

numbers on the tender, although in the course of time one had to peer very hard to realise they were in fact red; Stockport evidently being short of cleaners!

Returning to our morning visit to London Road, the up 'Mancunian' would be ready to depart at 9.45am behind a 'Prince' tank. Usually loaded to a minimum of 10 bogies, the train would take the Styal loop at Slade Lane Junction; on arrival at Wilmslow, the Longsight 'Scot' would be waiting to back on with the East Lancs coaches — two or three according to season. The 'Scot' would have run light engine from Longsight to Stockport, picked up the coaches and run forward to Wilmslow to await the arrival of the main train. Meanwhile, back in London Road the 'Pines Express' would be preparing for her 10.00am departure, a Crewe North working, for many years diagrammed for a 'Prince of Wales' 4-6-0. In those days Crewe North

Right:

Midland 0-4-4T No 1278 at Longsight shed in about 1933/34. Three of these engines at Longsight during the 1930s (Nos 1274/76/78) are believed to have worked locals out of Manchester Central when first built. No 1278 survived into BR ownership. Note the carefully stacked bunker. *W. Potter*

had a large stud of 'Princes' and one could watch this train for days on end without seeing the same engine twice. Indeed, I dare say that if one could also see the return 'Pines Express' at 4.50pm one might see the whole stud in a very few weeks.

The next important departure at 10.40am, the 'Sunny South Express', would be in the charge of an original 'Claughton' 4-6-0, for as long as they were available. During the morning there was a Stafford turn which was always headed by a 'Precursor'. At this time Stafford had nine or 10 of these engines, and they all took their turn on this job. An interesting arrival was a train which ran down the Styal line and was always in the care of a Shrewsbury 'Prince', often one which had been rebuilt with outside Walschaerts valve gear. The morning would end with the preparation for departure of the up 'Lancastrian' to London. This train travelled via Stoke-on-Trent and a 'Baby Scot' would be in charge, these being the largest engines allowed over the Stoke line at this time.

During the morning there would, of course, have been one or two arrivals on the MSJ&A platforms apart from the electrics from Altrincham. These

Top:

'Jinties' Nos 16427 and 16428 at Longsight in March 1934. These engines were built to a Midland design in 1926. Seen here with original livery and numbers, they were later renumbered 7344/45. *W. Potter*

Above:

Stoke (5D) Class 4P 2-6-4T No 2305 leaving Longsight for London Road in July 1936. *W. Potter*

would usually have been in the charge of LNWR engines; possibly the odd small tank engine but in the early 1930s an 'Experiment' 4-6-0 was the norm. It seemed the last survivors of this class usually ended their days at Warrington. I particularly recall *City of Chester, Scottish Chief, Buckland, Banshee, George Findlay* and *Bellona,* all of which lasted until 1935.

From mid-morning until late afternoon, when the city workers began their homeward trek, life in the terminus was less hectic and tank engine hauled local trains were much less in evidence. The 'Comet' would come and go from London and there would be one or two lesser London trains. Sometimes even a 'Compound' might have one of these, although in the main their work would more

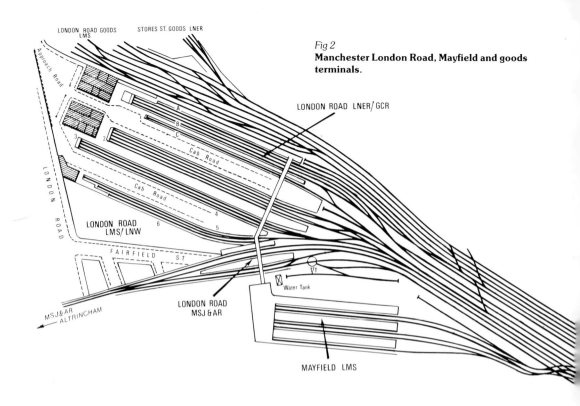

Fig 2

Manchester London Road, Mayfield and goods terminals.

often be confined to the West of England trains. These trains were always the poorest timekeepers, this being no reflection on the Compounds, time usually being dropped on the GWR! There was an interesting departure at 4.35pm from Platform 6 which ran non-stop to Crewe via the Styal line. This train consisted of only four corridor coaches and in my experience was always headed by a Monument Lane 'Compound'. Allowed only 30min to Crewe, I had long thought this train might afford a very interesting ride; accordingly I boarded the train one day and to my surprise found 'Baby Scot' No 5517 in charge. No 5517 was able to accelerate away from the service slacks with such ease that there were no fireworks and the ride was something of a disappointment. I recall another occasion when I boarded a train normally hauled by a Stoke 'Prince' tank and was pleasantly surprised to find No 5379 *Woodcock* rostered. On yet another occasion I recall a Stoke 'Prince' tank substituted by No 5466 *Glendower* and the driver finding himself in all sorts of trouble; he experienced the greatest difficulty in starting and even when moving to the centre road to pick up a van he had a fearful job trying to get a grip on the rails. The evening period was always most interesting. If one returned at about 5.30pm the 'Prince' which had brought in the 'Pines' might still be on hand, if not she would be back to work the 7.20pm Stockport-Crewe stopping service. Awaiting departure on Platform 6 would be a Stafford turn, again a 'Precursor', unlike the

morning turn however this would be the same engine for months on end. I particularly recall No 5281 *Erebus* having a very long spell on the train. At the same time on Platform 7 would stand a Rugby 'Prince' waiting to depart. This also would alas not afford a great deal of variety, over quite a long period of time I only recall two engines, Nos 5661 *Gallipoli* and 5665 *Suvla Bay*. The 'Claughton' which arrived with the 'Sunny South Express' would return on the 8.20pm Stockport-Crewe stopper and while Nos 5281 and 5665 were enjoying their spell No 5967 *Lance Corporal J. A. Christie VC* would likewise have quite a spell on this job. The down 'Mancunian' due at 8.00pm ran via Stoke and would of course be headed by a 'Baby Scot', followed in at 8.05pm by a Birmingham train which at this point in time would be in the charge of a Longsight 'Prince'; with 15 of the class at the local shed some variety could be expected here. Strangely enough, on the only occasion on which I rode on the train during these years a Longsight engine was in charge but she was not a 'Prince'. I had an excellent run behind No 5350 *India* (one of only three of the class to survive until 1948) — unfortunately destined to lose her name plates later when the name was given to a 'Jubilee'. Due in at 8.58pm was a West of England service behind a Longsight 'Compound', always late, sometimes behind the 'Lancastrian' at 9.15pm. This latter saw the return of the Longsight 'Scot' which had gone up in the morning with the 'Mancunian'. In my

earlier days of observing the London Road scene the local stud of Nos 6131 and 6165 to 6169 all took their turn on this working. No 6167 perhaps less than the others; maybe she was looked upon as being something of a 'Jonah' after her misfortune on a London express earlier in her career. During the mid-1930s No 6164 joined the stud and took over the job for several months. When No 6148 and then No 6156 came to Longsight, the same thing happened. After the ill-fated *Fury* had been rebuilt with a Stanier boiler and renumbered 6170 she settled down at Longsight and seemed to take over the job completely.

These were indeed the 'Golden Years', not least for the ordinary spotter. Train travel was at its zenith. Trains at holiday times frequently ran in two and even three portions, providing many gems for the notebooks. A Christmas Eve stands out in my memory — a cold, dank evening with a steady misty rain falling — just the setting for some spectacular bouts of slipping. A train is held at the signals just outside the station, the 'peg' comes off, the regulator is opened and the unmistakable sound of a LNWR exhaust follows; obviously in the hands of a real craftsman, No 5344 *Bloodhound* moves 12 packed corridors smoothly alongside the platform.

A strange and interesting product of the age was a train which arrived in Mayfield at around 9.00pm on a Friday evening, returning from London Road's Platform 3 at about 5.00pm on a Sunday afternoon. Unable to trace this train in the public timetable I enquired of the driver on one occasion and was informed that after the closing of the Newton Heath carriage works in 1932 a proportion of the work force had elected to work at Wolverton. This train brought home for the weekend those who had family still residing in Manchester. The train was known to local enthusiasts as 'The Bletchley' and it was usually hauled by a 'Precursor' from either Rugby or Bletchley shed. The first time I saw the train it was pulled by No 5300 *Hydra*; many were the rare 'cops' which appeared over the next few years. There were odd disappointments. Twice Camden's 'Compound' No 1109 turned up and No 5187 *Helvellyn*, for a number of years the last 'Precursor' at Longsight, finally moved to Rugby and was on the train the next weekend. Among the many 'Precursors' the odd rare 'Prince' or 'George the Fifth' also put in an appearance from time to time.

Certainly grand times for the spotter, one of my short early visits to London Road produced among other things *Hydra, Dragon, Felicia Hemans, British Empire, John Rennie, Gallipoli, Precursor, Vindictive, Planet, London Rifle Brigade, Private E. Sykes VC* and coincidentally *Comet* on the 'Comet' express to London. In the early part of 1933 the third division football club Walsall astounded most of the football world by beating the mighty Arsenal in the third round of the FA Cup, thereby unwittingly providing Manchester's North Western devotees with a treat. For in the next round Walsall were

Above:
Crewe North (5A) 'Prince of Wales' No 25627 *Lewis Carroll* **near Handforth with a 12-coach down excursion in June 1936. This locomotive was withdrawn a month later.** *W. Potter*

drawn away to Manchester City and two special trains brought their followers to Manchester. Walsall's two Princes, *Prince of Wales* and *Andromeda* had the jobs — rare indeed in Manchester were this pair in their latter days. Indeed, it was very likely their last visit, I have not come across anyone who saw them in Manchester after that date. Before the year was out *Prince of Wales* was withdrawn, one of the very first batch of 'Princes' to suffer this indignity, the others being *Conqueror, Hermione, Robert Southey, Charles Kingsley, Bret Harte, G. P. Neele, Admiral Jellicoe, Onyx* and *Tara.* The last named and *Bret Harte* were fitted with outside Walschaerts valve gear. *Andromeda* did not last much longer, she just about saw out 1934. The writing was now definitely on the wall, unsuperheated 'Precursors' had almost all gone, unsuperheated 'Experiments' were down to about 40 in number and most of those would not last much more than 12 months. Now a start had been made on the superheated engines. I wonder if we realised how quickly our other favourites among the LNWR passenger engines were destined to vanish. The 'Claughtons' would disappear fastest of all, except for the 20 fitted with the larger boilers. The unsuperheated ranks would be represented for a little longer by the 'Precursor' 4-4-2Ts and the

very occasional appearance of a 19in mixed traffic 4-6-0, the latter usually on the MSJ&A lines.

On the MSJ&A during the evening there would be a little steam activity. First on the scene soon after 5.00pm a regular Widnes working, for many years this would be a Fowler 2-6-2T working, Nos 6 or 8 with just occasionally No 7 turning up. Four other arrivals during the evening would be two Warrington workings, one Edge Hill and one Speke Junction working. The previously mentioned 'Experiments' often had the Warrington jobs, otherwise they would be 'George the Fifth' 4-4-0 workings, as would be the remaining two jobs. Other old stalwarts which ended their days on these somewhat sedentary Warrington turns were *Albatross, Bellerophon, Bactria* and *Berenice.* The Warrington 'Georges' to appear included *F.S.P. Wolferstan, Henry Ward, John Bateson* and *George Whale,* while from Liverpool one might expect *John Hick, John Rennie, John Mayall, S. R. Graves, William Froude, Edward Tootal, William Siemans* and *Richard Arkwright. John Rennie* had a tender from an ex-ROD 2-8-0 and had earlier been a Longsight engine for a period. If one of the 4-4-0 engines was withdrawn it was usually replaced at the shed by a similar engine as long as there were any still in traffic. One evening an interesting excursion from Walsall to Blackpool passed from the main line on to the MSJ&A line headed by No 5543 *Warwickshire* (Shed 8 Rugby) piloting unnamed Claughton No 5998 (Shed 10 Aston). The electric service to Altrincham was fast and frequent and continued until a late hour; electric services had commenced in May 1931 and needless to say the

average enthusiast took little interest in the service from that date forward. No doubt the city workers who used the service were well satisfied with the change. Initially the average journey time was cut from 27 to 24min and later to 21min. At Grouping the average time had been 30min worked by Great Central 'F1' 2-4-2Ts and LNWR Coal Tanks; occasionally the LMS substituted other types and latterly their contribution was the Fowler 2-6-2T. The diminutive tank engines must have found the frequent stops and tight schedules very taxing and it may be of some significance that several of the 'F1' engines which had been sub-shedded to Altrincham were among the first to be withdrawn.

An interesting service, almost forgotten today, ran over the line at Grouping. A train departed London Road MSJ&A at 10.25am for Euston. Calling all stations to Altrincham on prior notice being given to pick up passengers for stations beyond Northwich, and similarly at Hale and

Below:

Another Longsight 'Scot' No 6164 *The Artist's Rifleman* with Stanier tender, approaching Heaton Chapel in May 1936. *W. Potter*

Mobberley for stations south of Crewe. It stopped at Knutsford to pick up passengers for stations beyond Northwich, and after leaving Northwich stops were made at Middlewich and Sandbach. A luncheon car service was provided and the scheduled arrival time at Euston was 3.10pm. A return service departed from Euston at 2.25pm. Tea was served between Euston and Crewe, the service calling at Sandbach, Middlewich, Northwich, Knutsford and Altrincham to set down passengers from south of Crewe. Thence it called at all stations to Manchester to set down passengers from south of Northwich on prior notification to the guard. Arrival at Manchester Oxford Road was at 7.08pm and London Road at 7.12pm. A further service from Euston connected at Crewe with the 8.36pm for Manchester Oxford Road, having left Euston at 5.20pm. The connection due at Oxford Road at 9.55pm called at Sandbach, Middlewich, Northwich, Knutsford, Altrincham and Knott Mill, and all stations from Mobberley to Old Trafford on prior notification for passengers from Crewe and beyond. The Euston-Crewe train offered a dining car service. So far as I have been able to ascertain the two through trains did not run in 1926 but would seem to have operated in 1927. Between 1928 and 1932 they ran only between Manchester and Crewe where passengers had to change. After 1932 there was no service.

During the first half of the 1930s, besides the 'Scots' previously mentioned, Longsight had a

good supply of passenger engines on call. These included unnamed 'Baby Scots', Nos 5534/35/38/42/43/44 and 45 also *Private W. Woods VC*, *Private E. Sykes VC* and *Duke of Sutherland*. Also allocated were large boilered 'Claughtons' *Vindictive* and *Princess Louise*, 'Compounds' Nos 1105/06/10/11/18/21/56 and 58, 'Prince of Wales' 4-6-0 *Arethusa* and Nos 5690-5704 (three of which were named *Richard Cobden, Telford* and *Scotia*). Nos 5690/95 and 96 were withdrawn during 1934 and No 5699 moved to Rugby, as did the only 'Precursor' *Helvellyn*. 'George the Fifth' class *Sir Thomas Brooke, W. C. Brocklehurst, Elkhound, Coronation, British Empire, India* and *Canada*, also for a spell *John Rennie* and *John Mayall*. There was usually an old Midland '2P' engine either No 332 or No 356 — Buxton engines when not at Longsight; just what job they were intended for I failed to discover; whenever I saw them they were shunting around the shed yard.

One did not see a great deal of goods traffic at London Road, during an evening one would observe some activity in the yard and fitted goods trains would depart behind Willesden 'Crabs' in the 29xx series and another behind a Camden 'Baby Scot'; I recall one of the trains always had a GWR brake van. Usually one would also see an ex-LNWR 0-8-0 known locally as 'Fat Nancys' for some reason which I now forget. Not a great deal passed across to the MSJ&A. In the morning one might see the Altrincham pick-up, in early days probably a 'Cauliflower' or 0-6-0 coal engine would be in charge. Later Longsight received an ex-Midland '3F' for this job, No 3717 if I remember correctly. Now and again it might even be an 0-8-0. There would be the odd transfer job at Ordsall Lane on the Manchester Exchange line, reached by diverting

Below:
Webb 2-4-2T No 6699 inside Longsight shed in August 1935. *W. Potter*

at Castlefield Junction. Occasionally a small LNER job would appear from the CLC.

As I mentioned in the Introduction all was not always plain sailing. To my mind one of the strangest things concerning mishaps, accidents and the like is the high coincidence rate. From earliest times certain areas seem to have been unduly prone; for example around Penistone or the high reaches of the Settle line. Fortunately not involving loss of life were two incidents at Platform 4 within the space of about three months. At about 9.00am on 19 June 1924 a train from Macclesfield over-ran Platform 4, smashed through the buffer stops and demolished a wooden building, an up-to-date indicator and a clock. Incredibly there was no reported damage to rolling stock and only two or three passengers complained of slight injury. The driver was reported as saying he completely misjudged the distance. The only newspaper picture I can find is a rather poor one; it suggests the locomotive was probably a North Staffs 0-6-4T. If

Top:
'Experiment' No 5511 *Banshee*, date and location unknown. She finished her days at Warrington, outlived by a month by only five of her sisters. *R. W. Hinton*

Above:
Longsight 'George The Fifth' No 5348 *Coronation* at Edgeley in July 1935. Named for the coronation of the late King George V the nameplate bore the legend, *5000th ENGINE BUILT AT THE LOCOMOTIVE WORKS CREWE JUNE 1911*. *W. Potter*

the stationmaster and his staff had been surprised by that incident they must have been astonished on 26 September. Renovation of the area could scarcely have been completed when the 7.00am ex-Alderley Edge (calling all stations Stockport) consisting of 11 coaches drawn by an 'Experiment' 4-6-0 and again drawing in to Platform 4 gave a repeat performance, this time demolishing part of a clerks' office and part of a lavatory building. There was again no damage to the train and only one

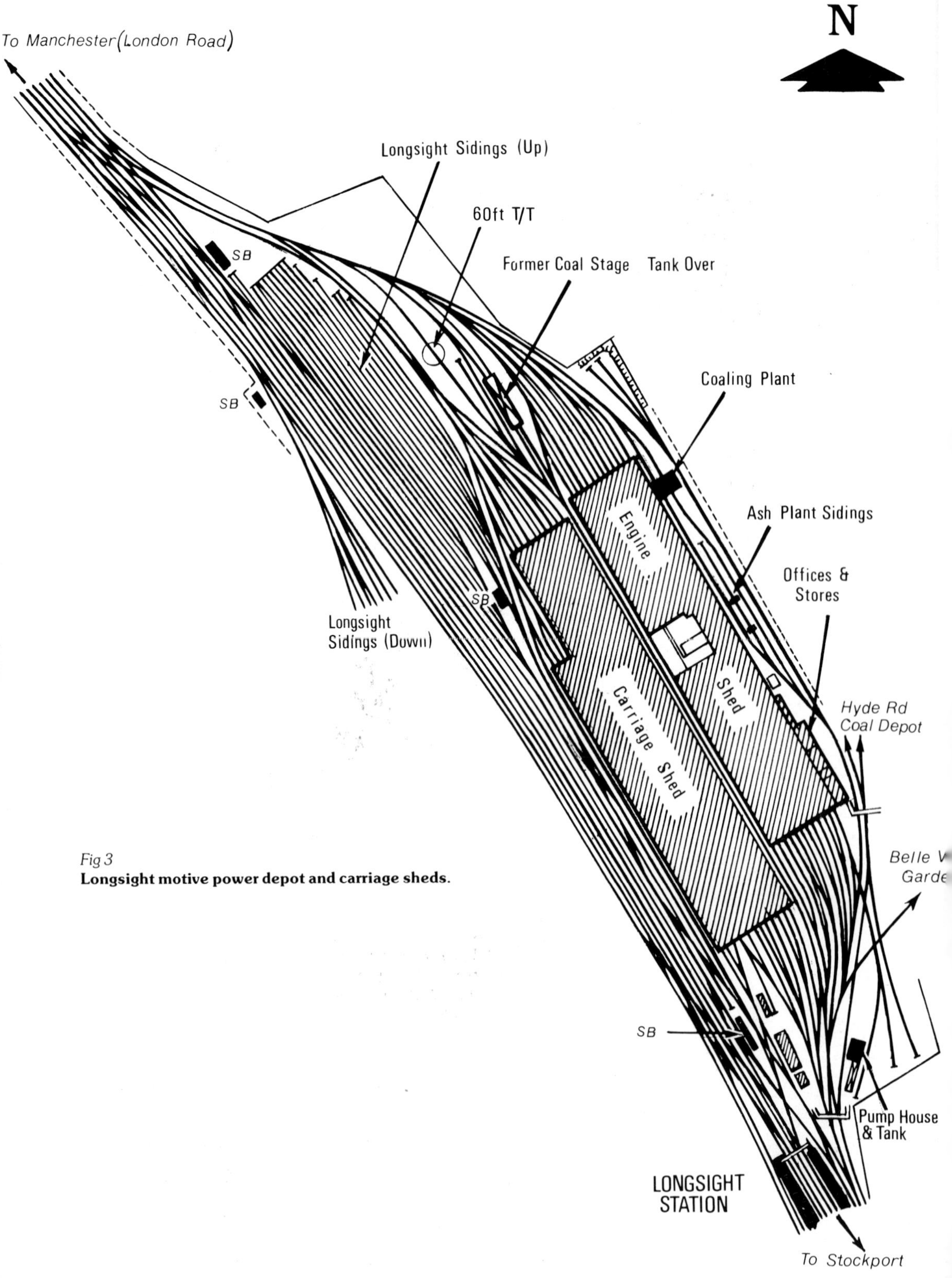

To Manchester (London Road)

N

Longsight Sidings (Up)

60ft T/T

Former Coal Stage   Tank Over

Coaling Plant

SB

SB

Ash Plant Sidings

Offices &
Stores

Engine

SB

Longsight
Sidings (Down)

Carriage Shed

Shed

Hyde Rd
Coal Depot

Fig 3
Longsight motive power depot and carriage sheds.

Belle V
Garde

SB

Pump House
& Tank

LONGSIGHT
STATION

To Stockport

Above:
Widnes 2-6-2T No 6, arriving at the MSJ&A platform at London Road with a train off the Lymm line. Date unknown. *W. Potter*

passenger complained of slight abrasions; one servant sustained injury to his head and was taken to hospital. Driver Walter Rogerson said he reduced speed to about 7 or 8mph when about 400yd from the buffers and to about 5 or 6mph when 200yd away. When he was four or five engine-lengths distant he thought he might pull up short so he partially released the brake; when one or two lengths from the buffers he realised he would over-run and applied full brake. Still not stopping he wound into full back gear and opened the regulator. He was only just moving when he hit the buffers and was astonished at the amount of damage. Guard Woolley had his handbrake partly on when passing No 2 Box because he considered the train to be running unusually fast. He then applied it fully and went to the vacuum cock. The train was one of his regular jobs and he knew the driver well — he did not usually run in at that speed. Acting platform foreman Walling said he thought the train was running rather fast when he first

Below:
A vintage shot at Crewe depicting large-boilered 'Claughton' No 5970 *Patience* piloting original 'Claughton' No 5930 *G. R. Jebb* on 26 May 1928. *R. W. Hinton*

sighted it. When about 50yd from the buffers the driver reversed his engine, it began to beat and sparks were flying from the chimney; before the collision the wheels were spinning backwards. Walling thought the speed at the moment of impact was about 10mph. There were other minor mishaps in the vicinity of the station. On 2 November 1927 an empty stock train collided with a light engine just outside the station and the engine and first coach of the empty stock train left the rails. Unfortunately it

Above:
Watford tank No 6904 approaching Timperley with a train for the Lymm line. Date unknown. *W. Potter*

Below:
A MSJ&A electric train near Brooklands in August 1945. *W. Potter*

was during the morning rush hour and considerable delays ensued. All was more or less back to normal by midday. At Ardwick Junction on 19 July 1929, large-boilered 'Claughton' No 5993 with a five coach train was run into from the rear by outside-geared 'Prince' No 5632 *Bret Harte* which was running light. The signalman at Longsight No 4 Box frankly admitted his mistake, saying it had been very busy and he had momentarily become confused between what had passed on the down fast and slow lines. *Some* responsibility was placed on the driver of the light engine. 18 September 1929 brought a morning of thick fog; at about 10.00am the late running 9.12am arrival from Buxton was routed into the wrong platform at Mayfield. Travelling very slowly, it collided with a light engine. There was no injuries and the only damage was one broken buffer. Another slight mishap occurred just outside the station on 10 July 1934 when two light engines collided; one was derailed and slight delays followed but there were no injuries.

Over the years the London trains seemed to have more than their fair share of misfortune. In one instance in particular the footplatemen must have experienced a particularly hair-raising few minutes without actually coming to grief. On 9 September 1936 the up 'Mancunian' which was travelling at speed near Madeley had a narrow escape from disaster. 10 miles south of Crewe an RAF, aeroplane crashed on the slow lines. Turning a somersault, the plane came to rest only inches from the passing express. The pilot was reported unhurt. With the use of fog signals the lookout man with a gang working nearby halted a train approaching on the up slow line, while the driver of the 'Mancunian' was successful in his endeavours to warn with his whistle the driver of a train approaching on the down slow line. The slow lines were cleared in about one hour. In fact the LMS was but five months old when the 11.50am Euston-Manchester express came to grief at Betley Road on 28 May 1923. A 439-ton train of 14 bogies drawn by unnamed 'Prince' No 1355 (5738) with 'Renown' 4-4-0 No 1947 (5174) *Zillah* as pilot was travelling between 65 and 70mph when the right-hand connecting rod of the 'Prince' fractured. The boiler was pierced both in the barrel and the firebox by the broken end. It was reported at the enquiry that No 1355, built at Crewe and turned out on 19 February 1920, had gone to Carlisle shops for general repair after 67,380 miles. It was stated that the engine was remembered in the works and that no fault was found in the connecting rod. After the works visit the engine was sent to Longsight shed in July 1922. The total mileage after leaving Carlisle to the time of the accident was 44,432. Following a similar accident at Cheadle Hulme on 28 April 1922, orders were issued for a special examination of connecting rods after an engine had run 20,000 miles. The last examination of No 1355 under this rule had been made on 19 February 1923 at which time the engine had run 30,550 miles without the rods having been taken down. On this occasion the rods were not taken to the bench, but were examined from below with a lamp. On 25 May the monthly examination was made and the rods were taken to the bench. It should be noted here that Driver Davies had reported both big ends knocking. Finally, on 27 May, the day before the accident, the rods were again examined by a different man who also found no fault. Between 19 and 27 May the engine had been reported four times for big-end or gudgeon pin knocking. The leading hand was not informed of the recurrence of drivers reports as the fitter was satisfied that there was no knocking and the driver was mistaken. It was subsequently found under tests and analyses that the broken rod was of inferior quality due to high phosphorus content combined with overheating during annealing. It was revealed that during the previous year (1922) seven cases of broken connecting rods had been reported on the LNWR (including L&Y), all on engines fitted with Joy valve gear. Many of the circumstances of the latest mishap, including the class of engine and position of the fracture, were identical with those of the incident at Cheadle Hulme some 13 months earlier. It was stated that a considerable number of these engines would have rods forged from steel manufactured under more up-to-date methods adopted since 1921 and that the danger of overstrain in these cases would thereby be considerably reduced. In the case of the 'Prince of Wales' class, strain was likely to be more severe than on other classes employed on long distance express work. The rod was short and stiff and with driving wheels of only moderate diameter the piston and valve speeds were consequently high. It is interesting to note that of 91 connecting rods condemned for flaws between May 1922 and May 1923, 80 were on engines equipped with Joy valve gear.

Although not strictly within the period covered by this volume, perhaps some further mention of the Cheadle Hulme incident would not be inappropriate. On 28 April 1922 'Prince of Wales' class No 877 (5645) *Raymond Poincare* was approaching Cheadle Hulme in the early hours of the morning with a four-coach train. A connecting rod broke and pierced the boiler and firebox. The first intimation of there being anything amiss on the footplate was an explosion and a violent blowback of scalding steam, hot water, red hot coal and ash. In the great tradition of footplatemen, the driver, although scalded and unable to see, nevertheless stuck to his post and brought the train to a stand. At this point he discovered the fireman was not on the footplate; climbing down from his engine, he met

Right:
Coal Tank No 27577 at Longsight July 1937, probably having come down the Lymm line. 20,000 was added to the numbers after 1934. *W. Potter*

the guard who was coming forward to ascertain what had gone wrong. The fireman was found on the track some distance back. Regrettably he died as a result of injuries to his head. It was stated later that the injuries were sustained when the man fell from the footplate, there being no way of determining whether he had in fact jumped from the footplate or had been blown off by the blast. *Raymond Poincare* was reported to have been frequently under treatment for motion trouble, demanding and receiving skilled attention on very many occasions. Since her appearance new from Crewe Works in 1915 she had run just short of 132,000 miles — 45,337 since her last overhaul. Subsequent shed movements of the locomotive tend to bring to mind the old adage give a dog a bad name. Ten days after this incident at Cheadle Hulme, 'Prince of Wales' superheater, 4-6-2T No 1710 (6983) broke a connecting rod at Furness Vale only a few miles away on the Buxton line. She had run only 17,000 miles since her last overhaul.

Over-running the platform was not confined to local trains, as witnessed by the occasion on 26 August 1924 when the 9.45am ex-London Road collided with the buffers on arrival at Euston. Several passengers complained of bruising received during preparations for alighting. In fact this came during a bad patch at Euston. Earlier in the same month an excursion train from Liverpool had collided with a light engine when entering Platform 3. Earlier in the year there had been a collision on the approaches to Euston involving a 'Scotch Express', a football excursion and an electric train.

On 2 October 1929 few passengers boarding the 6.05pm Euston-Manchester train could have imagined what a frustrating journey fate had in store for them. The locomotive, a large-boilered, Caprotti-valved 'Claughton', No 5975 *Talisman*, was soon in difficulty. She finally broke down

completely and came to a stand near Wolverton. A great deal of time appears to have been lost before a substitute engine arrived on the scene. Newspaper reports described the fresh engine, an 'Experiment' class unsuperheated 4-6-0, as not of the same power and speed as *Talisman*. Further time was steadily lost during the remainder of the journey and it was not until 11.40pm that No 5456 *City of Chester*, wended her weary way into Platform 4 at London Road , 2hr 5min late. The same train again ran into trouble on 18 April 1931 near Cheadle Hulme. This time the train came to a stand as a result of a fractured brake pipe. The time was 9.30pm and it would seem the train was running a few minutes late. There then appears to have been an inordinately long delay; Manchester, rather less than nine miles away, not being reached until 11.45am.

20 August 1934 saw the up 'Mancunian' divide passing Holmes Chapel. A newspaper report described the train as being nearly a quarter of a mile long, drawn by two engines travelling at 60mph. The train was recoupled and allowed to proceed cautiously to Crewe. There it was thoroughly examined before being allowed to go forward 65min late.

Driver Linley and Fireman W. Wood were working the down 'Comet' on New Year's Eve 1934. For a long time I thought maybe this had been Wilfred Wood VC after a whom a locomotive had been named. However Wilfred's son Harry believes this to be unlikely as he has no recollection of the mishap to be described. Driver Linley and Fireman Wood had 'Royal Scot' class 4-6-0 No 6167 *The Hertfordshire Regiment*. They had prepared the engine themselves and all seemed in order. Indeed they were passing Tring (31½ miles) before it was noticed that something was amiss. Hereabouts steam started to blow up between the front edge of the footboards and the back plate of the boiler. This situation gradually worsened and approaching Welton (70 miles) at a speed of 60mph there was a loud report and the footplate was suddenly enveloped in steam and hot water. Driver Linley stopped the train using the vacuum brake with the regulator still open. His right arm and wrist were badly scalded in the process. The two men left the footplate whilst they decided the best course of action. It was agreed Wood would proceed to Welton with a wrong line order with a view to obtaining assistance. Wood had his right arm scalded when he returned to the footplate to obtain the wrong line order form. The train eventually arrived in Manchester 2½hr late. Meanwhile the disabled engine had been taken to Rugby, but after it was discovered that one of the steadying bracket studs had blown out of the boiler backplate just below the level of the footplate, she was then taken to Crewe Works. Only five days earlier on Boxing Day No 6167 had sustained a similar failure when Driver Morcher and Fireman Aldridge were on the engine working the 1.30pm Euston-Carlisle. The stud came out of the same hole when passing Madely (150 miles) and in spite of the steam and water blowing into the cab Morcher was able to keep the train running until Wrine Hill intermediate signalbox was reached some two miles further on. There had been no previous escaping of steam and Aldridge assumed a gauge glass had failed. When groping for the gauge column cocks he received scalds to his left hand. Morcher escaped unhurt. Owing to shortage of steam they had taken on a pilot at Rugby; this engine managed to drag the train and disabled engine from Wrine Hill to Crewe.

No 6167 had left Crewe works as recently as 13 November after a general overhaul, during

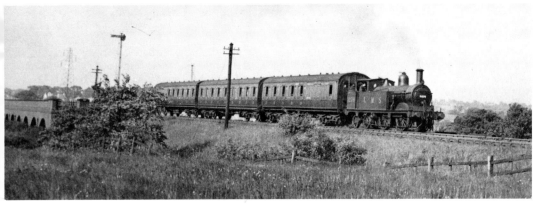

Above:
Midland 0-4-4T No 1278 working 'all stations' to Wilmslow via Styal in June 1939. The train is just leaving the arches over the River Mersey and the CLC line. The diminutive engine is dwarfed by the stock. *W. Potter*

Below:
'4P' 2-6-4T No 2381 working a local in the opposite direction and seen at the other end of the arches in July 1940. *W. Potter*

which the boiler was exchanged. The repaired boiler which was put on had been fitted with a new firebox wrapper and backplate. The steadying bracket on this class was fixed to the centre of the backplate below the level of the footboards by eight 1in steam-tight studs, arranged in two horizontal rows. The steadying bracket carried no weight and was intended to keep the boiler central between the frames, thus preventing lateral movement while allowing for longitudinal expansion. It was revealed that there was evidence of slack or poor workmanship when the engine was in Crewe Works and at Crewe North engine sheds; she had received treatment at Crewe North after the Boxing Day failure. There was criticism of several men and of the level of supervision.

There seems to have been some excitement on the 10.15am London-Manchester train on Sunday 6 February 1944. I have been unable to obtain sight of any official report and due to wartime economies local newspaper reports are very brief. It would seem however that quite soon after leaving London a fire broke out on the train. It would appear to have been first noticed a few miles north of Watford. A lineside observer was reported trying unsuccessfully to attract the attention of the driver by waving a

sack. A second observer ran to a signalbox and thereby had the train stopped a little further along the line. Evidently the crew were unaware of what was happening behind them. It was equally apparent that the passengers were only too aware. But why nobody thought to pull the communication cord is not clear. Two coaches were evacuated and removed from the train but the reports were conflicting; either the second and third or the third and fourth vehicles being those involved. The driver was reported as saying the fire might well have developed and spread further and quicker if they had been going at their usual speed at this point. Fortunately in the circumstances, they had been crossed from the fast to the slow line owing to repair work and were only doing about 15mph. Extra difficulty had been incurred in evacuating the passengers owing to the fact that one of the vehicles involved had the end vestibule door locked. This caused some concern and indeed a question was asked in the House on the subject.

Considering the high density of traffic along the MSJ&A tracks, about 120 passenger trains each way between 6.00am and 11.00pm if the Chester and Lymm lines are included, the line experienced remarkably few serious accidents. In thick fog on the morning of 6 December 1933 an electric train was put into No 2 platform at Altrincham at which an empty train was standing. Owing to the fog, Driver Charles H. Keatley of Altrincham did not see the empty train until it was too late to pull up. Driver Keatley was killed, there were no other casualties.

Below:
Bowen Cooke Class G2 'Fat Nancy' 0-8-0 No 9284 clattering along with a load of empties near Heaton Chapel in May 1936. *W. Potter*

Twice during January 1940 accidents occurred. A serious one in the black-out on the 10th at Stretford appears to have been largely the fault of a signalman. At 5.14pm the 4.55 electric service ex-Altrincham was standing at the platform when it was run into by the 5.01pm ex-Altrincham. A total of 23 passengers and three railway servants were injured, one passenger fatally. Previously the 4.48pm from Altrincham had passed Stretford at 5.02pm. There is some doubt when the next box (Warwick Road) gave 'Train out of section', but it seems not until 5.08pm. This had been followed by a steam train, the 4.15pm from Warrington. Driver Ratcliffe in charge of the Warrington train was brought to a stand by the Stretford home signal at about 5.05pm. Ratcliffe did not whistle in accordance with Rule 55 as he expected the signal to drop at any moment and in any case he was doubtful if the whistle would be heard in the box. Fireman Latham set out for the box after a short pause but the signal came off almost immediately. As they proceeded they received a wave from the signalman which Ratcliffe took as an indication that the advanced starter was 'off'. As the train moved forward Guard Jones noticed an electric train approaching about 100yd in the rear.

Motorman Langford on the 4.55pm from Altrincham, who had been brought nearly to a stand at Mersey Bridge (the next box in the rear), found the Stretford distant to be 'on' but, before sighting the home, saw the tail lamp of the steam train ahead. As the steam train moved away he observed the home was 'off', but nevertheless stopped at the signal. Guard Collier, not understanding why Langford waited although the signal was 'off', gave bell signals to Langford and walked to the front cab. Realising as he saw the tail light ahead that there had been two trains in section, he boarded the cab and they proceeded slowly into the platform where Collier alighted and called for the stationmaster. The collision occurred almost immediately afterwards. Motorman Ikin on the 5.01pm from Altrincham had passed the Stretford distant 'on' and the home 'off'. Running into the station at about 25mph he saw the tail lamp of the previous train when only about 50yd away from it. He made a full brake application but was unable to avoid the collision. Unfortunately, by this time a steam train travelling in the opposite direction had arrived and was standing at an adjacent platform with the locomotive underneath the road bridge at the west end of the platform. As a result the underbridge had become full of smoke and steam which prevented Ikin obtaining an earlier sight of the standing train. There were discrepancies between the registers at the Stretford and Mersey Bridge boxes.

The second incident occurred at Castlefield Junction, high on the viaduct near Knott Mill & Deansgate station. A goods train left the rails and demolished the signalbox. No casualties were reported but the lines were blocked for several hours.

During the blitz on Manchester of 21-23 December 1940 the viaduct was breached near

Above:
Webb 17in Coal Engine No 8271 inside Longsight shed in August 1935. *W. Potter*

Cornbrook. A steam shuttle service was introduced between Manchester Central and Warwick Road stations; the latter being preferred to Old Trafford for the change over point because of there being four platforms. The Cricket Ground (fast lines) platforms were used by the steam trains. The MSJ&A line had been quadrupled early this century between Sale and Old Trafford excluding those two stations. The shuttle service continued to operate until September 1941. Manchester Exchange was damaged during the blitz and it was possible to divert some trains at Ordsall Lane, via Castlefield Junction, to London Road MSJ&A, in the absence of the usual service at the latter place.

The CLC line between Tiviot Dale and Glaze-brook was joined at Northenden Junction by a LNWR branch from Edgeley. This provided the

Above:

Webb 'Cauliflower' No 8318 at Longsight in March 1934. Quite similar in appearance to the Coal Engine but with driving wheels 9in greater in diameter, a shorter chimney, larger splashers and an altered running plate, this one had also been fitted with a Belpaire firebox and 'Pop' safety valves. Over 100 of the two classes outlived the LMS. *W. Potter*

setting for a most spectacular mishap on 19 July 1927. A train of 35 wagons of coal was travelling from Edgeley to Liverpool. Approaching Cheadle, the only station along the branch, where only the coal sidings had been in use since 1917, the train divided on the level or possibly slightly rising gradient. Passing Cheadle the line gradient began to fall and the driver started slowing his train. The

Fig 4
Stockport station, locomotive depot and Adswood Triangle.

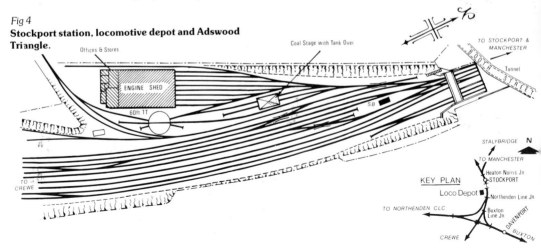

Above:
An interesting old stager at Edgeley in April 1936, a Johnson '2F' 0-6-0 rebuild No 3479. *W. Potter*

separated rear portion of some 20 wagons gathered speed, crashed into the front part of the train, telescoped several wagons, hurled two down the embankment and derailed several more. There were no injuries but coal was scattered far and wide. It is believed numerous villagers were able to make useful increases to their fuel stocks! The breakdown gang took six hours to clear the tracks which were used exclusively by goods traffic, apart from the odd excursion train which usually ran at weekends.

To conclude the tale of accidents I will mention a further wartime incident for which we will return to the main line. At 1.23am on 14 September 1941 the 12.35am Crewe-Leeds consisting of a four-wheel van and six bogies drawn by 'Baby Scot' No 5514 was brought to a stand at the home signal at Holmes Chapel. Driver Walsh sent Fireman Stoddard to the box immediately as a standing train is not visible from the box because an overbridge blocks the view. Before the fireman reached the box he could see the starting and advanced starting signals pulled off. However, he continued and reported to the box where, he said, Signalman Perks seemed surprised to see him and asked what he was. On being informed he then said 'I thought you were the Manchester'. No 5514 had travelled about half-way along the station platform at an estimated speed of 5mph when the train was struck from the rear by the 12.50am Crewe-Manchester consisting of nine bogies drawn by 'Prince' tank No 2395. Driver Hall on the tank engine alleged the Homes Chapel distant was clear for him but that he was slowing down for a speed restriction ahead. Driving on the right-hand side he could not see the tail light of the stationary train, the lamp being on

the left. His fireman was temporarily dazzled after firing and did not see the tail lamp either. There was some conflicting evidence between the signalmen involved and it was also clear there had been some confusion between them. The last coach of the Leeds train was demolished and the second last very severely damaged. Some 40ft of the next coach was smashed and the vehicle finished broadside on to the tracks. Six passengers including a goods guard were killed and 48 injured, of which number three subsequently died. No 2395 finished up on her side but the crew escaped with only trifling injuries.

Stanier engines play a rather small part in my personal story of London Road, it seems that I began to devote less time to this line soon after they really began to make their presence felt. Although in fact No 5020, resplendent in appearance turned up at Longsight on a Saturday afternoon when she was brand new, some time elapsed before this class began to appear regularly on Crewe turns. Initially in the shape of Nos 5027, 5029, 5047, 5049, and 5190 to 5198. The 5XP engines also began to come down from Crewe from the first. I recall seeing a number before they had received their names. A little further time passed before Longsight received their first allocation, although they had by this time taken one or two tank engines. As the 1930s rolled by Fowler 2-6-4T engines from Crewe North would arrive more frequently; no doubt a direct result of

new Stanier tanks being allocated to that shed, indeed the new engines also appeared. Of course the LNWR tender engines were disappearing from Crewe ever more rapidly, many, alas, to be cut up, the remainder to smaller sheds and doubtless more sedentary turns of duty.

By the outbreak of World War 2 LNWR engines had virtually vanished on the Crewe jobs as indeed they had from Longsight. However, 'Precursors' Nos 25292, 25245 and 25319 and 'Princes' Nos 25648, 25674 and 25725 continued to turn up from Stafford until well into 1940. No 5674 *Scott* had indeed been a Stafford engine for a good number of years, the others being more recent allocations. During the summer of 1940 ex-Midland Class 2P engines Nos 461 and 471 began to take their turn on these duties. It appears that quite a

number of Midland engines moved over to the Western Division at about this time, No 405 to Crewe for example, also one or two older 'Compounds'.

Stanier Pacifics must have a mention although this is a subject which has caused me considerable problems, not least because I myself never saw a Pacific in London Road before, during or after the war. Furthermore there does not seem to have been a great deal written on the subject in this context. The most recent reference I have come across being in an article in the November 1983 *Railway World* by Robert Griffiths. This article stated that BR 'Britannias' were the first Pacifics to be stationed at Longsight, but that Pacifics had worked into Manchester from time-to-time in LMS days when the absence of a turntable large enough to

accommodate them had necessitated a trip to the triangle at Adswood to turn. In fact it would appear that two of these engines were posted to Longsight during the summer of 1939 — several local recorders can confirm this and mention is also made in the *Railway Gazette*, *Railway Magazine* and *Railway Observer*. Generally Nos 6201 and 6206 would seem to have been the engines although one report suggests Nos 6201 and 6209. There is also a suggestion that they were intended to work the up 'Mancunian' and down 'Lancastrian' and the up and down 'Comet'. Memory may be at fault but I would have thought the 'Comet' was a Camden working myself. Evidently the move was not looked upon with great favour, both engines only remaining at Longsight for a short period; certainly they had moved away by the December. Peter

Helm has a record of a visit to Longsight on 15 November 1939 when Nos 6206/07 and 09 were on shed, the former bearing a Longsight plate. Peter kindly lent me his notes of late 1938/39 which indicate that the 6.45am ex-Crewe (all stations to Stockport, thence Manchester arrive 8.04am) frequently had ex-works engines in charge and a Pacific was used on numerous occasions. I have been unable to confirm further definite sightings during the war years although it seems likely they continued to appear sporadically. After the conclusion of hostilities they were again noted on the 6.45am ex-Crewe and on an afternoon turn which returned via the Styal line.

The first station out, Longsight, was the nearest station on the line to the famous Belle Vue Gardens. There was a single line from the shed

29

sidings leading across a field and into the gardens. From time to time engines and/or stock would be on display to members of the public visiting the gardens. These gardens contained a quite extensive zoo, a large fairground with all the popular rides of the day including a 'Big Dipper' roller coaster, a large ballroom and a hall which staged top class boxing and professional wrestling. Other attractions on Saturday evenings included speedway racing, greyhound racing and, during the autumn months, a firework display; all of which combined to draw a steady flow of excursion traffic on Saturdays and Bank Holidays. The first Saturday in September saw the annual crowning of the 'Railway Queen'; many special trains arrived at all the Manchester stations and usually something was put on show. I recall No 6125 *Lancashire Witch*, ex-works and resplendent in 1934. Included in the Groceries & Allied Trades Exhibition earlier that year in April, was a display organised by the LMS which included No 6100 *The Royal Scot*, a selection of the latest passenger rolling stock from all four companies and a strange four-wheeled van described as a vacuum cleaning van. This is believed to have been the only vehicle of its type, built originally for the Tilbury line.

Saturday 22 June 1935 produced one of Manchester's busiest days on record. The Independant Order of Rechabites held their centenary celebrations in the Belle Vue Gardens. It was estimated that 90,000 of the then current membership descended upon Manchester from every corner of the Kingdom. About 200 special trains arrived in the city and all their passengers were bound for Belle Vue. Considerable numbers were off-loaded at Hyde Road, Ashburys, Belle Vue and Longsight, but many more found themselves at the main city stations. Older readers may recall that Manchester employed boys to assist Tram Conductors on the eight-wheel bogie cars. On this Saturday every available roadworthy car was pressed into service along the Hyde Road and even the parcel delivery boys were detailed to act as trolley boys. Once inside the gardens the multitude consumed practically everything on offer, excluding intoxicants presumably. Special supplies of 7 tons of bread, 60,000 cartons of food, 120,000 bottles of mineral water and 60,000 gallons of milk disappeared as if by magic.

In April 1936 the LMS arranged something similar to 1934, on this occasion displaying No 5552 *Silver Jubilee*; again the four companies put examples of their coaching stock on show.

Sunday was a quiet day on the railway wherever one went and of course Manchester was no exception. There were a couple of up fasts in the morning usually worked by Camden 'Baby Scots', with a 'Royal Scot' now and again. The afternoon could be quite rewarding although far from busy.

An early arrival was usually a 'Claughton' in the early days, occasionally a strange one. The afternoon departure for London went through the usual pattern, large-boilered 'Claughton', 'Royal Scot' or 'Baby Scot' and 'Jubilee' as the years went by. I recall *Lancashire Witch* took the train in September 1934 after her visit to Belle Vue. The odd tank engine drifted in and out and there was an arrival on the MSJ&A. During the 1930s this was a Widnes working and as with their weekday job would usually feature 2-6-2Ts Nos 6 or 8, or just occasionally No 7. One memorable day it surprised us by turning up behind the ill-fated *Raymond Poincare* bearing a Preston shedplate.

Then of course there was the train back to Wolverton with its Rugby or Bletchley engine, and finally, very often after quite a long wait a London train due in at about 5.00pm. This could be relied upon to produce a 'Claughton' in earlier days, then a large-boilered 'Claughton' until the advent of the 'Jubilees'. This was a Crewe North turn and they might put a 'Scot' out just now and again but I cannot recall a 'Baby Scot', I rather think Crewe had no allocation of the latter type during the 1930s.

The other source of interest which turned up only occasionally and which is largely forgotten today was the theatrical special. Large touring companies would sometimes charter a train to move the entire show — cast, scenery, props etc — from one town to another, usually on a Sunday. I have heard it was not unknown for a circus to move by train also although I never saw one myself.

It is human nature to think ones own is best. Railwaymen almost without exception thought their line, their trains and their locomotives superior to the rest, and they were not slow to tell you so. Often they would be quite scathing about their competitors. Rare indeed was the Crewe driver with whom I had a conversation one Sunday afternoon. At one point he said 'Some of our chaps can remember the Webb "Compounds", those who cannot have heard lurid tales of their shortcomings. So you see, most are not prepared to give a Midland "Compound" a fair crack of the whip. But the truth is a Midland

Top right:
Lancashire & Yorkshire 0-8-0s came across to Stockport regularly. Seen here at Newton Heath in September 1938 is Aspinall unsuperheated '5F' No 12727, the only one of the class to outlast the LMS.
W. Potter

Bottom right:
Hughes superheater '7F' No 12952 which also lasted into BR days. August 1937. *W. Potter*

Right:
A nice shot of large-boilered 'Claughton' No 5975 *Talisman* **fitted with Caprotti valve gear, and a LNWR Longsight shed plate (16).** *Talisman* **came to grief with a 6.05pm London-Manchester train in October 1929, and seen here at her home shed with a 19in 4-6-0 behind. Date unknown.** *R. W. Hinton*

Below right:
The unfortunate 'Royal Scot' No 6167 *The Hertfordshire Regiment* **again appears to have trouble in the firebox area in this May 1936 shot inside Longsight shed. The 'Crab' is thought to be Buxton's No 2773.** *W. Potter*

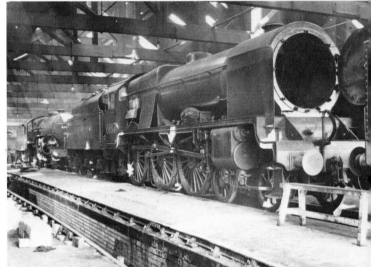

"Compound" will always beat a "Prince", a "George" now, that is another matter entirely'. It is said that Midland men alleged that a navvy could fire a 'George', a far more typical remark I would suggest.

Finally I feel it would not come amiss to devote a little space to three railwaymen who had by their gallantry during the first war, lifted themselves above we ordinary mortals. I refer to the three LNWR employees who won the highest award, the Victoria Cross. The LNWR to its credit named three of the latest express passenger engines in honour of these men. 'Claughton' class Nos 1407, 1097 and 2035 were fitted with plates reading, *L/Cpl J. A. Christie VC, Private W. Wood VC* and *Private E. Sykes VC.* Wilfred Wood and Ernest Sykes both came from within a few miles of Manchester and so far as I can ascertain the two locomotives which

bore their names were at Longsight at least until the outbreak of World War 2. After Grouping the engines were renumbered 5988 and 5976, and during 1926 they were transferred to Camden; the nameplates were removed at Longsight and attached to Nos 6018 and 6015 of the same class. Meanwhile No 1407 had become No 5967 and was also at Longsight, but she too moved to Camden, still bearing her nameplates. During 1933 Nos 6018 and 6015 were replaced by 'Baby Scots' bearing the same numbers but the following year they were renumbered, becoming Nos 5536 and 5537 respectively. I have found no evidence to support the theory but it is generally believed that No 5967 was not replaced by a 'Baby Scot' because 'Jock' Christie left the railway service after World War 1.

John Alexander 'Jock' Christie had been born in Edmonton, North London, on 14 May 1895 of

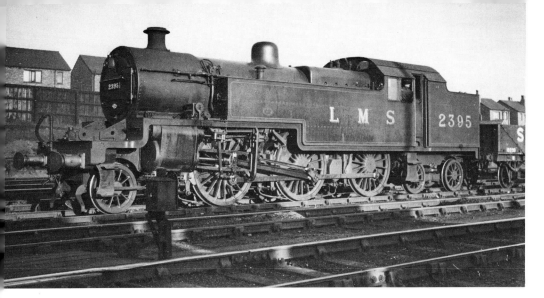

An unusual job with a class 'B' unfitted goods, for the ill-fated 2-6-4T No 2395, seen near Edgeley in July 1935. This locomotive, which was involved in the accident at Holmes Chapel in September 1941, was the first to appear with the side window cab. Some footplate men complained of excessive heat in this type of cab. *W. Potter*

Stanier 2-6-4T No 2540 with original domeless boiler is about to leave Longsight for London Road with empty stock in July 1936. *W. Potter*

Above:

A scene at Edgeley in August 1938 depicting both ancient and modern. Coal Engine No 8253 with 'Jubilees' No 5705 *Seahorse* in front and No 5733 *Novelty* behind. *W. Potter*

Right:

The unique vacuum cleaner van on display at Belle Vue in April 1934. *W. Potter*

Below:

In April 1936 it was the turn of Stanier's No 5552 *Silver Jubilee* to be exhibited at Belle Vue. *W. Potter*

Scottish parents. Serving with the 11th London Regiment he won his VC at Fejja, Palestine during the night of 21/22 December 1917. He advanced alone over an exposed position carrying explosives and was successful in destroying a Turkish stronghold which was attacking his unit. He later helped to break up another attack whilst under heavy machine gun and rifle fire. He relieved a difficult situation and undoubtedly saved many lives. Prior to enlisting, J. A. Christie had been employed in the accounts department at Euston. Some 10 years or so after the war he came to live in the Stockport area where he became a well known and respected member of the community. When he died in September 1967 there were four VC holders at the funeral.

Wilfred Wood was a Stockport man born on 2 February 1897. His working life was spent on locomotive duties in the area and he retired from a supervisory position at Stockport Sheds in 1960. Serving with the Northumberland Fusiliers, Private Wood won his VC at Casa Van, Italy on 28 October 1918. On two separate occasions he went forward alone, firing his machine gun from the hip, destroying two enemy machine gun nests and bringing back 300 prisoners. Wilfred Wood enjoyed a long retirement, and died on 3 January 1982.

Ernest Sykes was born in Mossley, near Stalybridge, in April 1885. Having commenced railway service as a platelayer at nearby Mickle-hurst, by the 1930s he was a passenger guard. After the war he was a well known figure in Stalybridge where he was Ticket Inspector. Also serving with the Northumberland Fusiliers, although not in the same battalion as Private Wood, Private Sykes

earned his VC for conspicuous gallantry and devotion to duty when his battalion was held up 350yd in advance of their lines near Arras on 19 April 1917. The battalion was under intense fire from the front and flanks and had suffered heavy casualties. Four times Sykes went forward under heavy fire and brought back wounded; going forward a fifth time under conditions which appeared to mean certain death, he remained tending wounded who were too badly injured for him to move. These gallant actions were performed under incessant machine gun and rifle fire showing utter contempt for danger. He died at Lockwood near Huddersfield in August 1949.

I am indebted to Wilfred Wood's son Harry for a remarkable and interesting little story from the 1930s. It seems that it would sometimes happen that Fireman Wood would have Guard Sykes on the train and at one of the local stations the Postman loading and unloading mail might be former Sergeant Joseph Lister VC. If there was a minute or two to spare one might have seen the surely unusual sight of three VC holders exchanging a few words. Joe Lister, who was born at Higher Broughton, Salford on 19 October 1886, had won his VC with The Lancashire Fusiliers near Ypres on 9 October 1917.

Below:
'Patriot' 4-6-0 No 45537 *Private E. Sykes VC* at Rugby in BR days. She appears to be allocated to Nuneaton at this stage of her life. *N. E. Preedy*

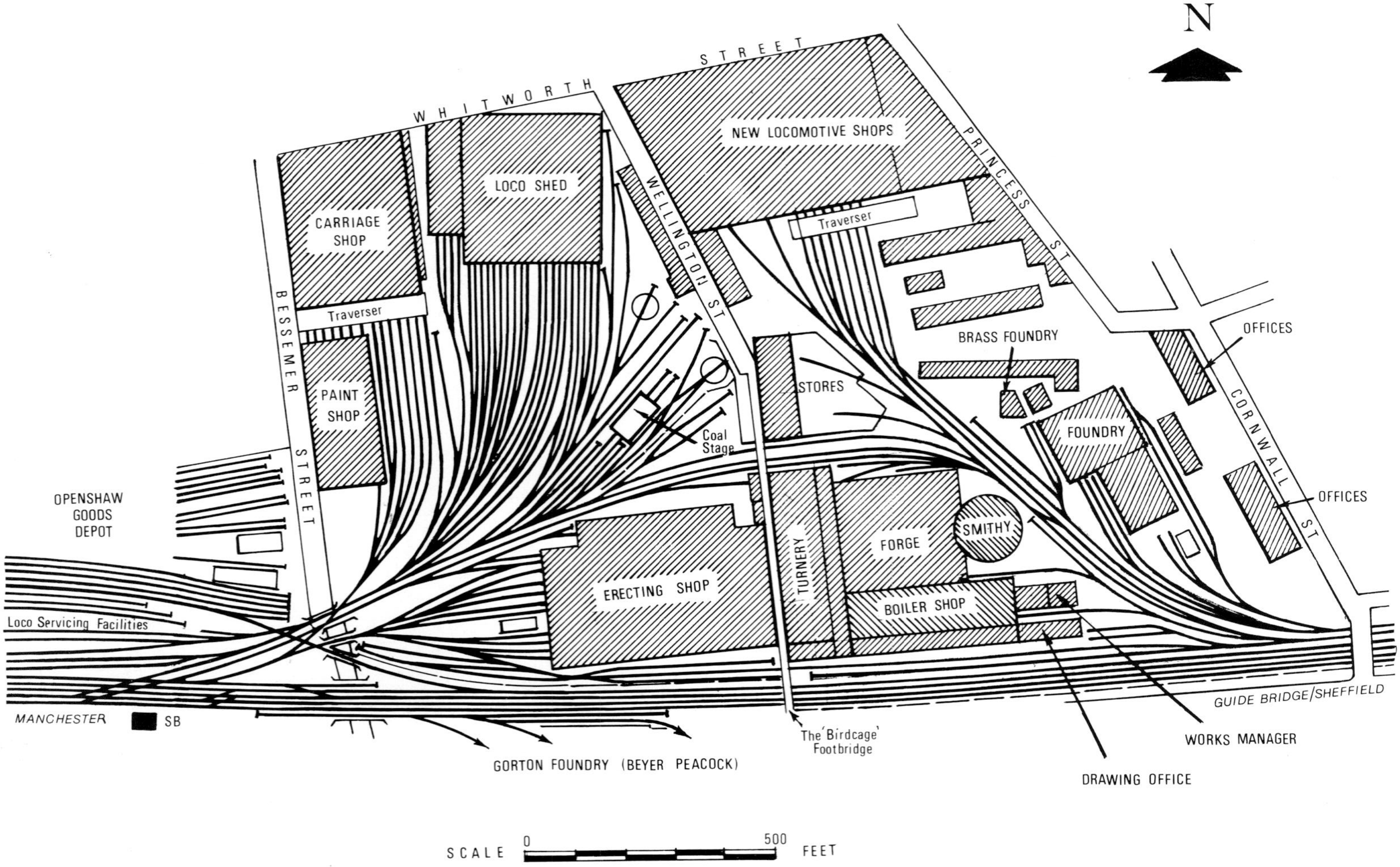

Fig 5
Gorton locomotive works and shed.

36

2 London Road

LNER

The LNER presence at Manchester London Road presented a rather different picture to that of the LMS. In the first instance it was and always had been the 'poor relation'. It had the most recently built line to London, although, let it be said at once, nowhere in the country was there a better constructed line for the running of express trains than the line from Nottingham Victoria to Quainton Road. Nevertheless Manchester London Road had only a handful of express trains and some of these were of a rather secondary nature. There was, however, a considerable amount of local traffic which created an impression of great hustle and bustle — an impression which was to some extent exaggerated, partly by the restricted accommodation making it necessary that all trains be dealt with as expeditiously as possible, and partly by the predominant make-up of these locals which consisted of sets of elderly gas-lit six-wheelers. These sets were close-coupled and the wheel beats always created the illusion that the train was moving at considerably greater speed than in fact was the case. Platform C, which was the longest platform, frequently accommodated two locals one behind the other.

Naturally the old Great Central had owned relatively few express engines compared with the LNWR and these engines continued to dominate the scene until well into the 1930s. Motive power variety was at a premium, which made keeping track of the movements of the various locomotives an easy task for the enthusiast. I have to admit to be something of a Great Central 'specialist'. On the credit side it must be emphasised that there was an excellence about the running of the Great Central trains which can seldom have been surpassed and which was to continue unabated until the outbreak of the war in 1939. There was also something about their locomotives which set them apart. I do not believe that locomotives have ever been con-structed better than those turned out from Gorton, especially during the reign of J. G. Robinson. As to their performance, it has become the general practice since the war to compare them unfavourably with most other engines, with the possible exception of the 'Directors'. This seems to me to be rather unfair; if one considers them objectively they compare favourably with their contemporaries.

Most of the express services into London Road were Gorton workings, although as the years went by there were some variations and alterations to diagrams; probably more than on the LMS lines. Until the summer of 1933 the top link jobs were generally in the charge of the 'Directors', in later years the 'D11' variety. 'D10' locomotives Nos 5429 *Prince Henry*, 5433 *Walter Burgh Gair*, 5434 *The Earl of Kerry* and 5438 *Worsley-Taylor* were at Gorton until 1933 at which time No 5434 moved to Copley Hill. The other three remained at Gorton until 1936, while others of the class were also at Gorton for short periods. Once the 'D11s' had become the established engines on top link jobs No 5433 was almost always the choice if it became necessary to utilise a 'D10', frequently appearing on London turns as late as 1934. During the period between the wars all the 'D11' engines except one had spells at Gorton. Nos 5504/07/10 did not appear on the strength after 1927 although No 5506 did have a short spell during the winter of 1928/29. No 5505 was at Neasden from new until the summer of 1947. In my experience an unusually long spell at one shed for a passenger engine, although numerous goods engines could probably match it. The Class B2 'City' inside cylinder 4-6-0s were usually to be found at Gorton until 1930, except No 5427 *City of London* which went to Neepsend towards the end of 1929, returning 12 months later. No 5424 *City of Lincoln* was also away for a couple of years from 1931; when she returned No 5427 was the only other representative

Below:

Gorton-based motor-fitted 'F2' No 5776 at Gorton in June 1938 with Stratford 'B17' No 2810 *Honingham Hall* behind. The 'B17' was ex-shops on 9 June 1938, noted on the Chester running-in turn on 16 June and on trips to and from Liverpool on 20 June. *W. Potter*

Bottom:

Wrexham motor-fitted 'C13' No 5191 awaiting shopping at Gorton in April 1938. *W. Potter*

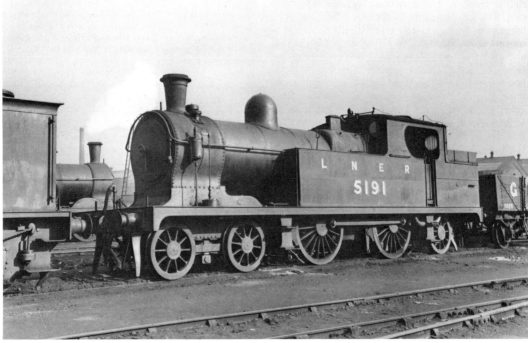

Above:
Langwith Class Q4 'Tiny' No 5067 awaiting shopping in April 1939. Note that the splasher over the centre coupled wheels has been extended to form a sandbox. A Kitson-built engine, No 5067 lasted into the BR era.
W. Potter

still at Gorton. These two had earlier had their cylinders lined up, an operation which evidently improved their general performance. No 5424 moved on to Lincoln in 1936 while No 5427 who also seemed to be something of a favourite remained until 1939, admittedly latterly employed largely on CLC after turning facilities had been improved at Liverpool. Class B3 'Valour' four-cylinder 4-6-0s Nos 6164 *Earl Beatty* and 6165 *Valour* had a spell in Manchester from 1927-1928 and Nos 6166 *Earl Haig*, 6168 *Lord Stuart of Wortley* and 6169 *Lord Faringdon* came to Gorton in 1933. The latter stayed for about two years, the other two (fitted with Caprotti valve gear) for about three years. They were employed on No 2 link duties mainly between Manchester and Sheffield over the difficult Woodhead line. The Caprotti engines were obviously preferred and put in a high mileage on these turns which they managed with ease with the usually light loads involved. Also on strength, until the advent of the 'K3' 2-6-0s towards the end of 1935, was a large stud of the four-cylinder 'B7' mixed traffic 4-6-0s. Normally about 20 strong they were frequently employed on No 2 link passenger turns and had a virtual monopoly of excursion and fitted goods traffic.

For a good many years the only 'foreign' express working I can trace was an up Marylebone on Tuesday, Thursday and Saturday afternoons, worked by the Neasden 'Director' which had come down to the Central station the previous evening with the 3.20pm down Marylebone. The 'Director' returned on the 2.20pm up, the Gorton 'Director' which went up on the other days took the 3.50pm. When the 4.55pm down Marylebone-Sheffield train was extended to Manchester in the early 1930s a Gorton engine picked up the job at Sheffield. After a short spell the diagram was changed and the Leicester engine came through to Manchester, returning with the 10.30pm up, thus providing the unusual sight at that time of a GC Atlantic in Manchester. This rare state of affairs continued until March 1936 when Leicester received their first allocation of Class B17 'Sandringham' 4-6-0s.

Local services operated to Glossop and Hadfield via Guide Bridge, to Romiley, Marple, New Mills and Hayfield or to Macclesfield Central via Guide Bridge and Hyde Junction or via the Great Central & Midland Joint line, diverging at Ashburys East Junction. There were also occasional services to Ashton, Stalybridge and Oldham Clegg Street or Glodwick Road, these latter comparing unfavourably with alternative LMS routes. The local scene was typified by a swarm of diminutive 'F1' and 'F2' 2-4-2Ts buzzing in and out like bees supported by the occasional 'C13' 4-4-2T usually on the Macclesfield service. Tender engines substituting on local turns were unusually 'J11' 0-6-0s or 'B9' 4-6-0s, although it was not unknown for ex-works passenger engines to appear. A stopping train to Sheffield at 3.52pm also quite often had an ex-works engine in charge. High above Dinting village in the Pennines was a triangular junction with a station variously known as Glossop & Dinting, Dinting for Glossop and finally plain Dinting; this was situated at the eastern end of the magnificent Dinting Arches viaduct. The 1-mile branch to Glossop (formerly Glossop Central) was served intermittently by a motor-train powered by an 'F1'. A motor-train might also be found working Guide Bridge to Oldham. On the Macclesfield line extra services between Macclesfield and Bollington

Below:

Only when ex-works would one see a 'Tiny' in this condition. Mexborough's No 6181 is on Gorton yard in April 1936. Note the splasher extended over the three rear pairs of coupled wheels. Built at Gorton in 1911, No 6181 was eight years younger than No 5067, but was withdrawn March 1939, *R. W. Hinton*

were worked at one time by Sentinel Steam Rail Car No 43301 *Commerce*, the car could usually be seen at Gorton on a Sunday when it attended for servicing. Unlike the LNWR the GC never had any qualms with regard to working tender engines tender first on passenger trains.

A very great deal of the GC section traffic was goods and mineral; coal trains in particular could be regularly observed queueing up one behind the other in the loops over the Pennines. The huge marshalling yards at Mottram were hives of industry after opening in 1935, other spots of continuous activity being Dewsnap, Guide Bridge and Ardwick: relatively little coming through to London Road.

In earlier times the Manchester, Sheffield & Lincolnshire Railway, the forerunner of the Great Central, had suffered more than its share of accidents, having a particularly bad spell during the 1880s; most tragically at Bullhouse in 1884 where 24 persons lost their lives and Hexthorpe in 1887 which resulted in 25 deaths. There had been improvement since that time and with one exception nothing really disastrous happened in the immediate Manchester area during the period under review. Unfortunately there was some loss of life in connection with a mishap in the up Woodhead tunnel. I recall a collision in fog at Fairfield involving a local drawn by a 'C13' tank but have failed to uncover any reports of the incident. There were two relatively small mishaps at Godley Junction. On 15 February 1934 in fog a goods train on the main line struck with a sideways blow a number of trucks in a goods train on the Tiviot Dale line. Some derailment occurred which caused delays to services, but no injuries were reported. On

22 November 1936 the Sunday 5.30pm down Marylebone, which was due at London Road at 10.15pm, suffered considerable delay when the leading bogie of the first coach left the rails. Passengers no doubt endured much frustration, the train not restarting until 1.00am on the Monday morning. However, no injuries were sustained.

The early hours of 10 October 1935 brought a most spectacular incident at Dunford Bridge, as a result of which traffic on the line was subject to considerable delay. In the still small hours the driver of a part fitted Colwick to Deansgate goods train was travelling along the down loop approaching Dunford Bridge, misread a signal and crashed into the bufferstops when he had expected to rejoin the main line. The engine, 'B8' 4-6-0 No 5004 Glenalmond came to rest heeling well over to her right, fouling the main line. Almost immediately the down mail, drawn by 'B7' No 5476, passed by at speed sustaining considerable damage to engine and train in the process. Needless to say the impact did not do No 5004 a lot of good either and both engines had to be towed to Gorton works. The goods train was laden mainly with produce for the market and a fleet of lorries made the journey from Manchester to convey the goods to their destination.

It used to be said with some justification that watches could be reliably set by the 9pm arrival from Marylebone at Platform A. Alas on 14 February 1936 things went sadly awry. Persons meeting the train would have been surprised to learn that she was 10 minutes late at Sheffield. Worse was to follow and one wonders if the tardy arrival at Sheffield had any bearing on subsequent

events. Immediately after entering Woodhead tunnel and surmounting the long climb from Sheffield, loud strange noises were heard and a full brake application was made. It transpired that the engine had deposited part of her motion on to the track. No derailment followed and although the engine was completely enveloped in escaping steam the crew escaped injury. The excellent alarm system in operation in the tunnel ensured that the signalmen at Dunford and Woodhead were alerted and the section was closed at once. Passengers were assured they were in no danger and the only inconvenience they suffered, apart from a long delay, was a sharp and rapid drop in temperature as the breakdown affected the steam heating. Restaurant car attendants supplied hot tea and coffee, and some biscuits. One and a half hours elapsed before an engine was attached to the rear to draw the train and its disabled engine back to Dunford Bridge. There was yet further delay before a suitable engine arrived to take the train on to its destination. Over many years I have made enquiries to discover which engine was involved, a Leicester Atlantic would have been expected and No 5267 of that shed turned up at Gorton works a few days later with casualty damage, it seemed a reasonable assumption she had been the culprit. However quite recently, and from two separate sources I

Below:
Also a rare sight was a ROD '04' 2-8-0 in such resplendent condition as Mexborough's No 6195 seen here at Gorton after shopping in May 1935. *W. Potter*

The usual appearance of goods engines, Gorton's '04/4' rebuild No 6287 on the turntable at her home shed. Note the unusual single-window arrangement on the cab sides. *R. W. Hinton*

ave heard that in fact 'D10' 'Director' No 5433 *Valter Burgh Gair* was the engine involved. It is a matter for conjecture how a Gorton engine came to e on the train.

A not uncommon occurrence on Sundays was the closure of the up Woodhead bore for roof inspection and other maintenance work. The up ne continued to climb steeply throughout almost the entire length of the tunnel and in consequence the roof suffered far more than that of the down bore from the pounding exhaust. Interruptions in the down bore were as a result less frequent. When as occasionally happened a bore had to be closed on a weekday, every effort was made to reduce delay to passenger services to a minimum, some of the goods traffic quite often being diverted via Huddersfield and Stalybridge.

Without doubt one of the most unfortunate accidents in the area took place on the morning of Sunday 29 July 1928. In the Ardwick district of Manchester there was a short line connecting the LNER main line with the LMS line from Manchester Victoria. On this short stretch of line the accident took place at Midland Junction. A chartered excursion train from Hull to Blackpool had travelled down the LNER line, diverted right at Ashburys West Junction, right again at Ancoats Junction, the distance between the two junctions being a mere 270yd. A further 335yd further on is the Ancoats Junction starting signal with the Midland Junction distant on the same post, 565yd beyond which is the Midland Junction home signal guarding the junction. The excursion train stopped at the Midland Junction home signal, the usual practice for LNER trains going forward into LMS territory, and the point at which an LMS locomotive would take over the train, and an LMS guard would replace his LNER counterpart. The rear of the LNER train was 345yd beyond the Ancoats Junction starter.

The excursion train passed Ancoats Junction at 10.31am. At 10.33am Signalman Gurney at Ancoats accepted a light engine from Ashburys West but did not pull off, intending to allow the light engine to proceed as far as his starting signal under Rule 40. He watched the approach of the light engine, and when it was between 50 and 60yd from his home signal, travelling at about 10mph he pulled off the home signal. He considered the speed reasonable and, assuming the driver knew he would have to stop at the starter, he took no further action. Both driver and fireman maintained the Ancoats home signal was off when they were between 150 and 200yd away from it. Subsequently Gurney saw that the light engine had not stopped at the starter showing danger and sent the 'train running away on right road' signal to Midland Junction. Now there was little the signalman at Midland Junction could have done to avert the disaster.

The light engine had come off Belle Vue shed on to the Great Central & Midland Joint line, had joined the Great Central main line at Ashburys East Junction and was on its way to Manchester Victoria to pick up a train for Derby. Driver Wilson said that after passing through Ashburys station he had been brought to a stand for a minute or two at Ashburys West Junction. After leaving there he saw that the Ancoats home was off and could see that the starter was off also, but not the Midland Junction distant, that was on. A sharp shower of rain came on as he was passing Ancoats junction and he took his coat from its hook and draped it around his shoulders. He did not notice the starter and distant again although he passed right underneath them. Soon after this he saw the Midland Junction home off. (Actually for the excursion train.) He assumed therefore he had a clear road, he was running at about 15mph when he became aware of the LNER train an engine length away. He immediately closed the regulator and made a full brake application, he managed to reduce speed to some extent but could not avert the collision.

It was pointed out that the light engine — Johnson 4-4-0 No 356 of 1883, rebuilt first by Deeley and then by Fowler in 1923 — was right hand drive and running tender first (as a result of which the driver was on the outside of a sharp curve) and that the line was on a viaduct, the wall of which would give a poor background liable to render the excursion train inconspicuous.

No 356 had the very low Midland tender and a newspaper picture taken immediately after the crash does not indicate a very high pile of coal, although of course some could have been scattered after the collision. What the fireman was actually doing as the engine travelled around the curve is not clear. A newspaper report quoted him as saying 'The crash happened before I knew the train was there and I cannot remember anything about it. I was flung on one side of the engine and my driver was bruised about the face'.

The driver of the train engine, which had uncoupled, drawn forward, reversed over a cross-over and was running back to Gorton shed, saw the light engine approaching and said to his mate 'Hold on for God's sake, it is going to bang into us'. He added 'It hit the back of the train, there was a tremendous crash, woodwork shattered, I pulled my engine up just in time to prevent running into wreckage which fouled our line'. A total of 30 passengers received slight injuries but none of these were detained in hospital. The majority of passengers elected to carry on to Blackpool in a second train brought up from Manchester Victoria. The guard's van No 2378 took the brunt of the impact and LMS Guard Albert Edwin Shallcross of Salford was killed; LNER Guard James Millford of

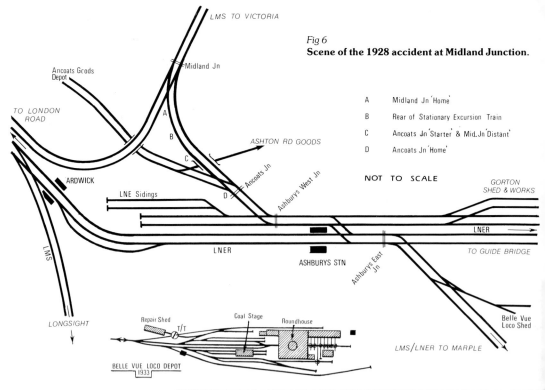

LMS TO VICTORIA

Fig 6
Scene of the 1928 accident at Midland Junction.

Midland Jn

Ancoats Grods Depot

TO LONDON ROAD

A

B

ASHTON RD GOODS

C

A	Midland Jn 'Home'
B	Rear of Stationary Excursion Train
C	Ancoats Jn 'Starter' & Mid.Jn 'Distant'
D	Ancoats Jn 'Home'

ARDWICK

Ancoats Jn

Ashburys West Jn

NOT TO SCALE

GORTON SHED & WORKS

LNE Sidings

D

LNER

LMS

LNER

TO GUIDE BRIDGE

ASHBURYS STN

Ashburys East Jn

LONGSIGHT

Repair Shed
T/T
Coal Stage
Roundhouse

Belle Vue Loco Shed

LMS/LNER TO MARPLE

BELLE VUE LOCO DEPOT
1933

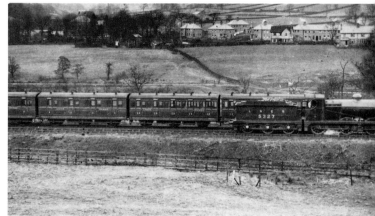

Above right:
Gorton unsuperheated 'J11' No 5327 in old-style livery at Hayfield in 1926. Note the close-coupled six-wheel stock.
W. Potter

Right:
Gorton 'B7' No 5462 in grimy wartime condition pounds up towards Woodhead with a train of empties in about 1945. Note the new pattern cylinders fitted in 1937. *W. Potter*

44

Below:

he view from Gorton coaling tower in April 1936. The Midland's Belle Vue shed is in the foreground, a Midland '4F' is at the coaling stage, and a LMS-built

'4F' nearer the camera. The Great Central & Midland Joint line curves away in the background. Belle Vue Loco Football ground is behind the depot. *W. Potter*

Doncaster was injured about the head and died in hospital in Doncaster 20 days later.

The Derby train for which the light engine was intended would have been the 11.35am calling only at Marple at 12.03pm and Chinley at 12.20pm, arriving at Derby at 1.22pm. At Chinley there was a connection for stations to Sheffield via the Dore line at 12.55pm and at Derby connection was made with the noon train from Manchester Central at 1.45pm which called at Leicester and St Pancras, and with a train for Trent, Beeston and Nottingham.

There could not have been many passenger turns out of Belle Vue, indeed I do not recall there being any by the early 1930s. On Sunday mornings the lines around Ashburys were very lightly used, and it is likely that the crew of the light engine were accustomed to running down to Victoria without let or hindrance and were not expecting another train in their path: familiarity does after all breed contempt. However their being stopped at Ashburys and checked at Ancoats should surely have indicated some obstruction ahead. Of course they denied the Ancoats check. It has been written of accidents that in some cases men have seen what they expected to see rather than what was actually there to be seen. It seems to me that this may well have been the case in this instance. If, as he says, the driver saw that the Midland Junction home was off, should he not have seen something of the excursion train standing at the signal? There must have been the movements of two engines in front of

the train, surely there must have been some sign, smoke or steam? Naturally in the circumstances Driver Wilson and Fireman Bland were held to be largely to blame, but the Inspecting Officer also criticised Signalman Gurney for not bringing the light engine to a stand at his home signal.

The first 'B17' locomotives posted to Gorton were intended for working the Liverpool to Harwich Boat Train between Manchester Central and Ipswich. By the summer of 1933 the number of 'B17s' at Gorton was sufficient to enable them to be put in the No 1 link. Let it not be said without some misgivings, however. The enginemen did not like them, chiefly because they gave a very uncomfortable ride, something GC men were not accustomed to; but also because there were those who had doubts about the small Great Eastern pattern tenders carrying sufficient coal for the London run. This was peculiar, there being little difference to the Ipswich run. In both cases the coal had to be carefully stacked to a considerable height above the top of the tender. It was said that during the early stages of a run it was inadvisable to stand near the platform edge of a suburban station when a 'B17' was passing through at speed as there was always the likelihood of pieces of coal being thrown off. This was something I have never witnessed myself, but, having ridden immediately behind the tender and observed the violent oscillation whereby the cab of the engine appeared to be moving from side to side and up and down at the same time, some of this movement inevitably being transferred to the

45

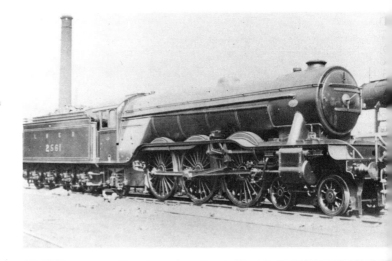

tender, I have no difficulty in believing the stories of falling coal.

In view of the antipathy of the Gorton and Neasden men towards the class there was some surprise at the way the men at Leicester took to them from the start. I know my view does not make me very popular with the older GC enthusiasts but I do not find this very remarkable. The Leicester men had struggled on with only the 'C4' Atlantics for many years and to me that is the answer. In the same way I am unable to accept the popular view that they were good looking engines. They were not too bad when viewed from the front, but from the side, everything looked as if it had been pushed up to the front end. The driving wheels appeared to be too close together and there was a great gap between the rear driver and the trailing wheels. There are several stories to account for their being

nicknamed 'Jersey Lilies': the two most common being that they were so named after either the music hall artist Lily Langtry; or a very large and ungainly barmaid in a public house near Gorton. As for myself I should think the latter!

In the autumn of 1938 one or two Pacifics and 'V2' 2-6-2 locomotives appeared on the scene and went into the No 1 Link. Later on Thompson's 'B1' 4-6-0s arrived. When I returned home after the war they were very well established and I must say always gave a good account of themselves in my experience. The Pacifics which arrived in 1938 were not the first to be seen at Gorton. In 1924/25 one or two had been sent there for running in, of which a small number of photographs do exist.

Sundays on the LNER side of London Road station were if anything quieter than on the LMS.

46

There was a remarkable early morning train to Cleethorpes which called at all stations which were open and took almost six hours to complete the journey. For example in 1924 it departed at 5.40am, stopped at all stations except Ardwick, Fairfield, Woodhead and Neepsend, and arrived at 12.30pm. It was allowed 117min from Guide Bridge to Sheffield, whereas the 5.25am weekday train which called at all stations was allowed only 106min for the same stretch! Purely local traffic was so sparse as to be almost non-existent, there were only two trains each way to Glossop for example, although there were one or two connections at Dinting.

What London traffic there was on a Sunday departed from Central. There was one arrival at London Road at 10.23pm (later 10.15pm). There was one reasonable train to Sheffield at 4.50pm; this was a No 1 link turn, the engine going forward to Marylebone with the 5.35pm ex-Central. There was provision for hikers with a service to Hayfield which was augmented during the summer months,

Above:
No 6165 *Valour* at Sheffield Victoria, on Armistice Day, year unknown. *Great Central Railway Society Collection*

Below:
Woodford 'B5' 4-6-0 No 5180 awaiting shopping during the 1930s. *W. Potter*

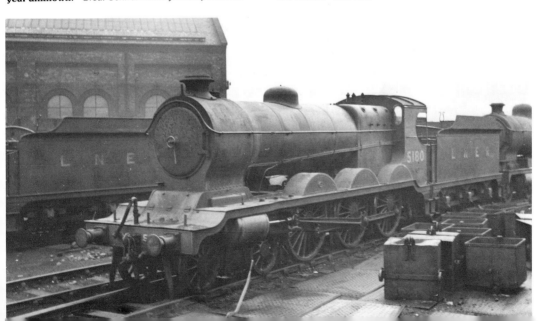

and about four trains each way on the Macclesfield Central line.

During the summer months there would often be one or two half-day excursion departures. Excursions during weekdays mostly departed from Central where there was more space available, and frequently connected with trains from Liverpool and Warrington. Indeed in later years excursions would often start at either Liverpool, Warrington or occasionally Irlam, cross over to the MSJ&A at Cornbrook Junction, pick up at Oxford Road and then run through the London Road MSJ&A station before crossing over to the LNER tracks.

During the summer of 1927 improvements and alterations were authorised for the LNER side of the station. These were to include a new entrance, enlargement of the booking and baggage offices, provision of one central barrier to the three platforms and the construction of a new buffet, ladies waiting room, general waiting room and bookstall. These facilities would replace the old

which were to be demolished. A new gentlemen's lavatory and hairdressing salon would be opened beneath the concourse.

1929 saw the first of the new Manchester district 'Variety' posters. I understand that similar posters had been on display in London for some months. At first glance these posters looked exactly like posters used by Variety Theatres; presumably on that score they were calculated to make the casual observer take a second glance. The display and coloured inks appeared identical with the theatre posters. In the first instance arrangements were made for the posters to be displayed in hotels, cafés and hairdressing establishments as well as at LNER stations, offices and agencies. Whether or not they

Left:
Ex-LD&ECR 'J60' 0-6-0 No 6410, on duty as works shunter in June 1938. *W. Potter*

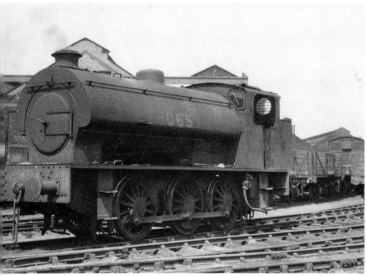

Left:
'J94' 0-6-0ST No 8065 at Gorton in July 1947. *W. Potter*

Left:
An unusual visitor to Gorton Works in postwar days, Mersey Electric Railway No 3 (Ex-G. E. 'J66' No 7297). *W. Potter*

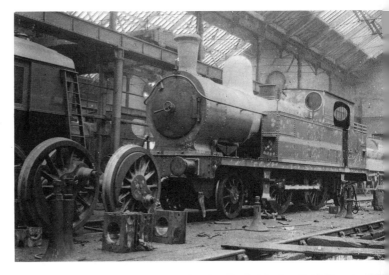

Right:
'F1' 2-4-2T No 5583 inside Gorton Erecting Shop in June 1934. No 6168 *Lord Stuart of Wortley* is behind with a CLC railcar ahead. *W. Potter*

Below right:
Putting the finishing touches to new 'B12' 4-6-0 No 8576 at Beyer Peacock's yard in September 1928. *W. Potter*

were very successful I cannot say. I only remember them vaguely which leads me to suppose that in Manchester at least they could not have lasted for very long.

For many years the War Memorial engine No 6165 *Valour* would be seen at Gorton at the beginning of November. On 11 November, suitably decorated with poppy wreaths, she would work the 8.20am up Marylebone.

As already indicated J. G. Robinson's engines were all of good sound construction, very solid in appearance compared to some one could think of, and exceptionally well turned out. Almost without exception they were very sure footed. I have gone over to Sheffield on a train that called perhaps at Dinting or Hadfield and a 'Director' would restart without any difficulty. The 'B2' and 'B3' engines could move quite heavy loads from a stand without any slipping and rapidly work up a good speed, which doubtless accounted for the popularity of the former class on the Lincolnshire lines where stops were frequent and the terrain flat. The 'B7' was the King of them all, capable of moving considerable

loads without the slightest difficulty even when starting against an adverse gradient. Robinson's tank engines, also of quite imposing appearance, were generally capable permormers, although it has been said that the 2-6-4T was inadequately braked for goods work. The excellent 4-6-2T on the other hand was evidently good enough for Sir Nigel Gresley to have built a further batch for use in the Northeast, as indeed he did with 'Directors' for Scotland.

Perhaps Mr Robinson's goods engines were the most generally successful of all his designs. He started with a further batch of the already established 'J10'. Large numbers of these engines spent many years on the CLC where they seem to have been universally popular, especially at Heaton Mersey where I had the opinion that the enginemen were quite happy with a 'J10' on any of the work available from that shed. The 'J11' must have been as good a 0-6-0 as one was likely to find anywhere in the country. The larger 0-8-0 and 2-8-0 engines were solid and unspectacular in appearance but always masters of their tasks. One assumes that

Mr Robinson could hardly have imagined that examples of his 2-8-0 design would find their way to the other side of the world and indeed, in Australia, outlast those in this country.

In 1930 the 4.55pm Marylebone-Sheffield train was extended to Manchester London Road. Initially a Gorton engine took over the train at Sheffield, the *Railway Magazine* for July 1931 devoted a little space to the working of the train between Sheffield and Manchester. Some enthusiasts might have been a little surprised to note the best time had been put up by a 'B7'.

Strangely enough Gorton engines suffered one very obvious defect which 'The Tank', as the works was known locally, never managed to remedy. They all suffered to a greater or lesser degree from burnt smokebox doors. If one accepts the theory that such burning is a result of ill fitting doors one would have expected Gorton to have come up with an answer. One seldom if ever saw a Midland engine with this disfigurement and rarely a LNWR example either, although the latter might very well be enshrouded in steam which would appear to be escaping from every possible point. Other engines around Manchester which one might observe with burnt smokeboxes were Great Northern goods engines and tanks, and occasionally one of the older Lancashire & Yorkshire types.

Across the tracks from the locomotive works at Gorton was situated the premises of the Beyer Peacock Company, noteworthy perhaps for the building of locomotives for overseas railways, especially Garratt types. In earlier days they had built numerous engines for the Great Central, including Atlantics, several types of 4-6-0 and goods engines. During LNER days several of the Great Eastern 'B12' engines were constructed by Beyer Peacock and fitted with Lentz Poppet Valves. Also constructed there, was the famous Beyer Garratt.

An interesting pairing which would have made a grand sight in earlier and cleaner days. 'C1' No 4454 and 'B1' No 5195 storm up towards Woodhead in May 1945.
W. Potter

3 Victoria

Dating back originally to 1844 Manchester's Victoria station had on two occasions been extensively enlarged and rebuilt. Originating with one of the smaller companies, by Grouping it was the headquarters of the Central (L&Y) division of the LNWR; the two companies having amalgamated in 1922 thus anticipating events. By this time the station had 16 platforms, Nos 1-10 of which, at the eastern end of the station, were terminal and used solely by local trains. With the exception of No 11 the through platforms were on curves which grew progressively more severe, No 16 being very sharp indeed. Boarding and alighting could thus present something of a problem to the elderly or infirm. The station was also equipped with an ingenious overhead 'railway' which conveyed parcels, luggage and the like between the various platforms in large wicker skips. It may well be that childhood impressions have a lasting subconscious effect, for I always had a feeling of foreboding, not enjoying the hours I spent there as much as I ought to have done. I can only conclude that this stemmed from my first visit. My family had moved to Manchester from Leicester when I was an infant and my earliest memories are of Central station and trips to Leicester. I enjoyed these trips immensely and developed a great affection for Central station. It was decided we should go to Blackpool for a week at Whitsun in 1925. Accordingly, I found myself on Platform 11 at Manchester Victoria for the first time on a wet and dismal Saturday morning. I can still recall looking eastwards, we seemed to be trapped in a dark and gloomy cavern at the foot of a steep hill. I now know this hill to be Miles Platting Bank, rising for over a mile at a gradient of between 1 in 47 and 1 in 59. Then the train came in and compared most unfavourably with what I had become accustomed to expect on the Midland, both as to motive power and passenger accommodation. An elderly looking 0-6-0, with a five-figure number was in charge of a collection of small, uncomfortable, hard-riding non-corridor bogie vehicles. On reflection it seems likely that being a holiday weekend the train was either a duplicate or an excursion. Also with hindsight I now realise the train took the route via the Wigan line diverging at Dobbs Brow Junction to regain the Chorley-Preston line. Just by the way, it rained every day and it was a long time before I saw Blackpool again! The return journey on the following Saturday was altogether better, our transport being a train of decent corridor stock drawn by an imposing red monster of an engine which even put my beloved Midland 'Compounds' in the shade.

Again childhood impressions have a lasting effect, for I always had a fondness for the Hughes 4-6-0. Whatever may have been said or written about them subsequently, at the Grouping they were the pride of the L&Y and if talking to old drivers of that era harsh criticism is not recommended. The majority of the final total of 70 were not built until 1923-25 so whatever their faults they were not worn out with years of slogging. Perhaps I was lucky, I had numerous rides with 'Dreadnoughts' as they were known in Manchester, and I never found anything to complain about. Particularly impressive were a couple of eastbound departures from Victoria which I experienced in the mid-1930s, one of which went up the bank to Miles Platting, the other around the loop to Thorpes Bridge Junction, where although the gradient is slightly easier, there is the added handicap of a very severe left-hand curve almost off the end of the platform. On both occasions the load was 12 bogies and on both occasions banking assistance was spurned. In each case the climb was achieved without any slipping and with no obvious difficulty, albeit at a rather steady pace. In my experience a banker would have been taken even with the most

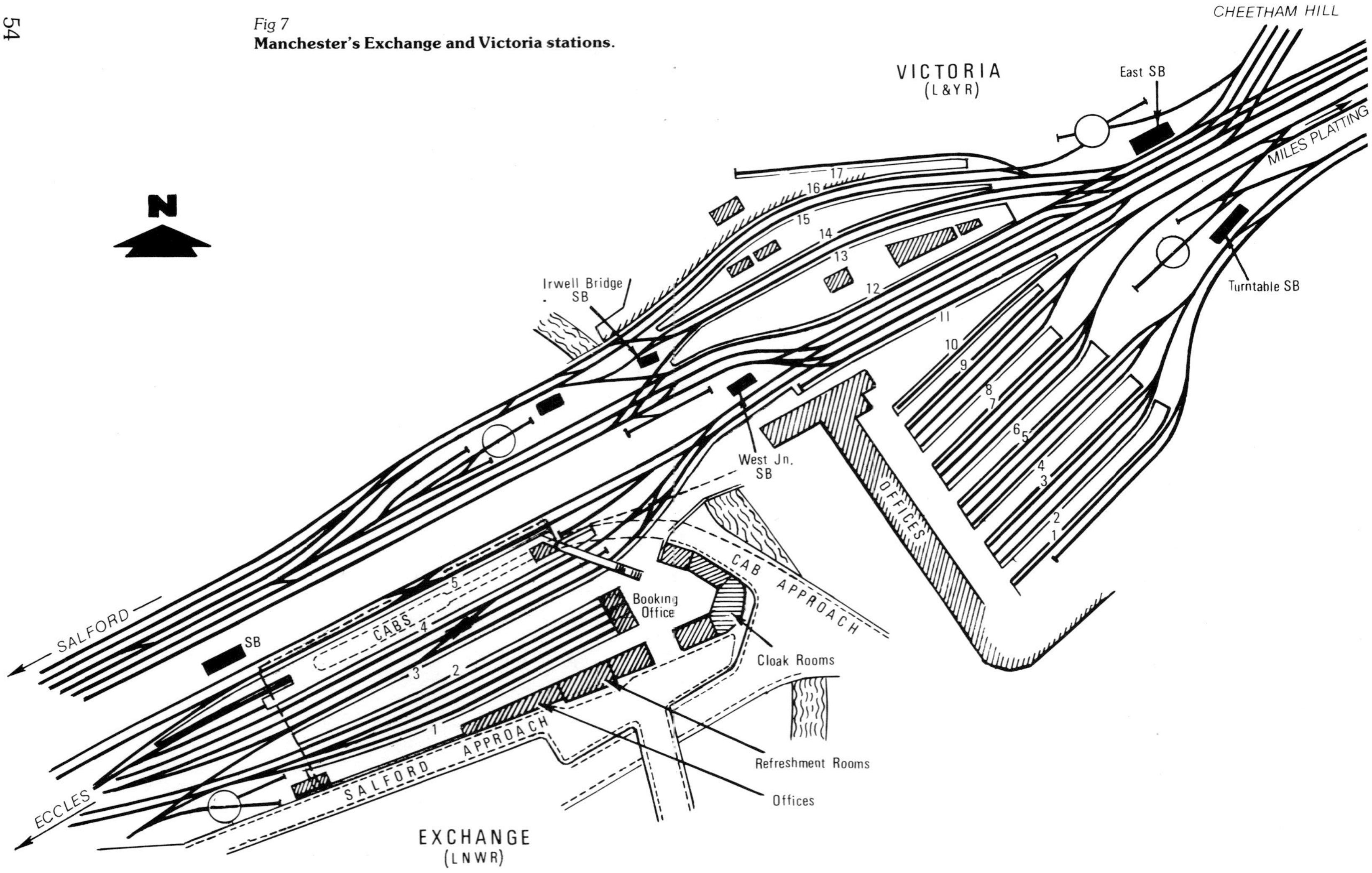
CHEETHAM HILL
VICTORIA
(L&YR)
East SB
MILES PLATTING
Turntable SB
17
16
15
14
13
12
11
10
9
8
7
6
5
4
3
2
1
Irwell Bridge
SB
West Jn.
SB
OFFICES
CAB APPROACH
Booking
Office
Cloak Rooms
CABS
5
4
3
2
1
SB
SALFORD
ECCLES
SALFORD APPROACH
Refreshment Rooms
Offices
EXCHANGE
(LNWR)
N

Fig 7
Manchester's Exchange and Victoria stations.

modern engines. Until the mid-1930s they were most prominent in Victoria. Then under Stanier they were decimated, their number reduced to 11 by the end of 1937. Then there was something of a reprieve until No 10464 went in June 1939. Doubtless the remainder would soon have followed but for the war. As it turned out Nos 10412/23/29/32/37/42/46/48/55 and 10460 saw the war years out appearing regularly on the Blackpool-Manchester run. A friend of mine who served in the RAF in Blackpool at one period of the war had notes which revealed all 10 in regular employment. On leave in Manchester in 1945 I made two trips to Blackpool and was delighted to have Nos 10429 and 10455 in charge of the train. However, on the return journeys a 'Black Five' and a 'Jubilee' were turned out. During 1949/50 I had occasion to make frequent visits to Preston on a Sunday afternoon and very often a 'Dreadnought' was at the head on the outward journey. Finally, in 1951, I attended a conference in Blackpool and on the outward journey had my last ride behind one of my old favourites, the sole survivor, No 10455, shortly before she was withdrawn.

Notes of my earliest visits to the L&Y have alas failed to survive, but memory tells me the 4-4-2 'Highflyers' were still to be found for a number of years after Grouping. They were not a favourite of mine, to me they seemed awkward and ungainly. There were also a few 4-4-0s which I do not recall seeing in traffic, but I recall one being dismantled at Horwich. I do however recall my second visit to the Fylde Coast, some years after the first. On the outward journey we had 'Prince' No 5754 Dalton and returned behind 'Crab' No 13025.

Below:
Hughes 'Dreadnought' rebuild No 10409 at Platform 12 at Victoria, awaiting the 'off' for Blackpool in March 1939. Note the small tender and the Horwich practice of mounting 'Pop' safety valves transversely. No 10409 lasted for only three months after this picture was taken. *W. Potter*

Bottom:
No 10455, a Blackpool favourite until the very end, was the last to go in 1951. It is seen here at Newton Heath in May 1935. *W. Potter*

Above:
Unsuperheated Aspinall '2F' 0-6-0 No 12411 at Agecroft in August 1937. *W. Potter*

It was at about this time that I began to make occasional observation visits to Victoria. Two of my strongest memories are of the line of engines (usually L&Y 0-6-0s) awaiting their turn to bank a train up the gradient, and of an occasional LNWR section train bound for Leeds storming through the centre road with a banker in the rear also pounding away furiously. The L&Y 0-6-0s were built and rebuilt in considerable numbers between 1887 and 1922, with some variation as to size, detail and valve gear. In common with most British engines of this type they led long, active and useful lives, and were frequently to be found on passenger work, especially in the early days when they were a common sight charging along to the coast sporting express lamps. Something in the order of 500 were taken over by the LMS and over 300 lasted into the British Railways era. In my younger days the LNWR trains were usually banked by a Patricroft 'Precursor' which filled in as Exchange station pilot when not engaged in banking. Latterly a 'Black Five' acted in this role, initially No 5059 appeared to have the job on a regular basis, until eventually she was replaced by No 5141.

Throughout the LMS era the commonest sight in Victoria, and indeed at most places on the Central Division must have been the Aspinall and Hughes 2-4-2T engines. These sturdy little locomotives were not only very free running, for their size they were able to tackle and keep time with quite heavy loads, particularly the larger '3P' variants of the class. For many years they tackled the difficult road to Oldham, 48 trains each way daily, until eventually they were largely superseded by Fowler's 2-6-2T.

Even after the appearance of the Hughes Baltic tanks some of the shorter distance express trains were still in the charge of the little 2-4-2Ts. They still held their own on some routes after Fowler's fine 2-6-4T came on the scene. Like the 'Dreadnought' they so closely resembled, the 'Baltic' tanks were reputed to be both very hungry and very thirsty, the main thing against them I believe was their size and power. There just was not sufficient suitable work available. Nevertheless during the 1930s one would expect to see at least half of them if one spent an hour or so at Victoria. For example on 3 February 1936 Nos 11111/12/13/14 and 11115 were noted and on 6 March Nos 11110/12/13/15 and 11119. 'Prince' tanks on view would usually be the later ones with side windows and doors with droplights fitted to the cabs, and numbered in the 24xx series. At the same time an earlier one would very likely be found having worked down from Stockport. Before Stanier's engines arrived on the scene the express turns which were not worked by the Hughes 4-6-0s were usually worked by LMS-built 'Compounds' or 'Prince of Wales' engines of the later unnamed series. 'Compounds' appeared from Newton Heath, Blackpool, Southport, Bank Hall, Low Moor and Wakefield. Newton Heath had a number of the 'Prince of Wales' class at one time, including two named ones, Nos 5753 *Premier* and 5754 *Dalton*. Others selected at random from my notes are Nos 5792/93/94/99 from Wakefield or Normanton, Nos 5803/04 from Low Moor, and Nos 5838-44 from Fleetwood. No 5736 *Disraeli*, one of a batch at Patricroft for many years, had a short spell at Agecroft. The '2Ps', mostly LMS-built, were part of the scene. During the winter of 1935/36, Nos 564, 585, 588, 589, 602, 614, 651, 652, 662, 676, 682, 683 and 690 were noted: some were local, others worked down from Hellifield. Also observed were Midland-built engines Nos 412 and 474, the former off the Great Central and Midland Joint line, the latter from Hellifield. Other regular visitors from the Hellifield line were ex-Midland '3P' engines Nos 728, 731 and 732. A heavily laden departure for the East Lancs line soon after 5.00pm would, at one time, be headed by a '2P' piloted by a radial tank. Very much part of the scene during the 1930s were the Horwich 'Crabs'. A generally popular engine, they might often be seen on semi-fast turns and were always well to the fore on excursion traffic. During this period Newton Heath had three 'Baby Scots', Nos 5546/47/48; these worked turn and turn about with Nos 5549/50 of Polmadie on the Manchester-Glasgow turns. In 1937/38 Nos 5546 and 5548 were named *Fleetwood* and *Lytham St Annes*.

Inevitably the old order had to give way to the new. I believe I am correct in saying that the first Stanier locomotive at Newton Heath was 'Black Five' No 5078. It chanced that on the first Sunday after her arrival I had arranged to take an excursion to Leeds Central via Sowerby Bridge; I was expecting a 'Crab', indeed on the previous occasion when I had used the train we had the original, No 2700. On this occasion, however, we were given the 'new' engine. In a short while the 'Black Fives' were a part of the daily scene all over the Central Division, most of the sheds with passenger workings having an allocation. The 'Jubilees' came on the scene rather later and the percentage of their numbers to be found on the division was always less than that of the 'Black Fives'. Newton Heath and Blackpool had an early allocation. As indicated earlier Blackpool remained true to the 'Dreadnoughts' for as long as they were able, the new engines being used on their main line turns largely. So far as I recall the Newton Heath 'Jubilees' did not usurp the 'Baby Scots' from the

Above:
Hughes rebuilt large-boiler '6F' 0-8-0 No 12782 at Newton Heath in August 1937. This unsuperheated type originally built by Aspinall is similar to No 12271 which ran away down Miles Platting Bank on New Years Day 1936. *W. Potter*

Below:
Hughes-rebuilt Aspinall 0-6-0 No 12445, taking water at Agecroft in September 1937. *W. Potter*

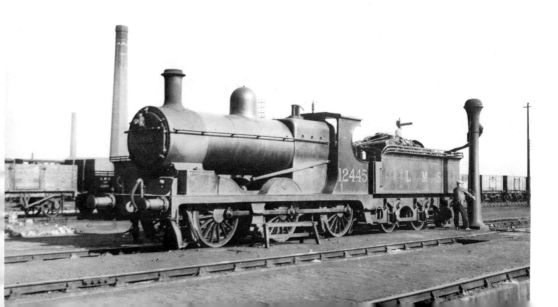

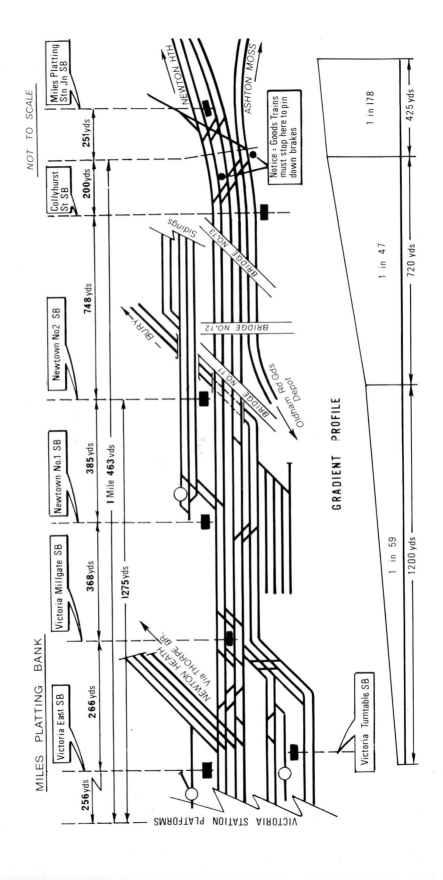

Fig 8
Miles Platting Bank.

NOT TO SCALE

Miles Platting Stn Jn SB

NEWTON HTH

ASHTON MOSS

Notice : Goods Trains must stop here to pin down brakes

251 yds

200 yds

748 yds

Collyhurst St SB

Newtown No2 SB

BRIDGE NO.13

Sidings

— BURY —

BRIDGE NO.12

BRIDGE NO.11

Oldham Rd Gds Depot

385 yds

1 Mile 463 yds

Newtown No.1 SB

Victoria Millgate SB

368 yds

1275 yds

MILES PLATTING BANK

NEWTON HEATH via THORPE BR.

Victoria East SB

266 yds

256 yds

VICTORIA STATION PLATFORMS

Victoria Turntable SB

GRADIENT PROFILE

1 in 178

1 in 47

1 in 59

425 yds

720 yds

1200 yds

Glasgow trains. I had an interesting and exhilarating run behind Polmadie's No 5549 in June 1938; 25min were lost before Carstairs, largely regained by the time Wigan (North Western) was reached and then lost again to Manchester. The train was routed via Tyldesley and Eccles and we were put in behind either a local or a goods at Tyldesley.

The Stanier tank engines also made their appearance in Victoria in due time. Small numbers of the 2-6-2T variety appeared on the locals. Although the Fowler 2-6-2Ts had a poor reputation generally, I believe they more than held their own against the newcomers on the arduous Oldham and Bacup lines. Rather more of the new 2-6-4T engines turned up and whilst I cannot now be certain I think they must have taken over some of the heavier turns worked by the 2-4-2Ts.

One of the interesting sights was the Blackpool Club train, with its special Club Cars for the businessmen. I understand that the members each had their own particular seats and that the windows did not open. There were also Club trains to Windermere and Llandudno, the latter using Exchange station. There were also Boat Trains to Fleetwood and Heysham. The evening departure of the latter was usually a must for spotters during the 1930s. Earlier Platform 11 had been extended and joined with Platform 3 at Exchange, making what was claimed to be the longest platform in the world. Beside the section between the two stations from about 8.30pm onwards the stock of the Heysham Boat Train would be standing. Much of the mail and parcels, etc would be loaded before the passengers began to arrive. Over a long period the engine would be a Carnforth 'Compound', certainly it continued to be so during my time as an observer. I recall two of the old 'seven-footers', Nos 1006 and 1008, all the remainder were LMS-built so far as notes indicate (Nos 1117, 1123/24, 929/30/31) — others may have also appeared at one time or another, I rather think Nos 1073/75, 1126/27 and 1171.

Not a great deal of goods traffic passed through the station during the hours of daylight. There were several yards in the close vicinity; in particular I must mention the Salford yard west of the station. This yard was at street level, the railway passing alongside on a viaduct. The yard was quite extensive and at one point was bisected by a busy street, rail traffic being shepherded across by a flagman. Access to the yard was by a steep incline from Oldfield Road Junction. This approach being from the west, trains from Yorkshire were able to approach by travelling via Bury, Radcliffe and Clifton Junction. Salford yard was shunted by 0-4-0ST engines with 3ft driving wheels giving a very short wheelbase. These midgets might also be found in the other yards, where they were assisted by six-coupled saddle tanks which Aspinall had

rebuilt in the 1890s from Barton Wright 0-6-0 tender engines, some of which dated back to 1870; these had 4ft 6in drivers. Such goods traffic as might be seen passing through the station would usually be in charge of eight-coupled tender engines; the three L&Y varieties and Fowler's LMS-built engines. A through goods on the LNWR section would most likely have a LNWR 0-8-0 for motive power. I cannot recall ever having seen a goods come down the loop from Thorpes Bridge. It may well be that owing to the severe curve at the foot of the bank, loose coupled trains were always routed via Miles Platting. In the event of a runaway down the loop line the results at the foot of the bank could have been catastrophic. They could be quite spectacular running away down the straight from Platting, as I shall relate.

Before dealing with accidents and mishaps at Victoria, I should mention the new and improved signalling installations involving both Victoria and Exchange. To reduce to a minimum the disturbance which is inevitable when such work is undertaken the work was done in two stages. During the night of 9/10 March 1929 the L&Y lines were converted. The Westinghouse Brake & Saxby Signalling Co Ltd installed new power signalling. All apparatus worked satisfactorily with only a few minor delays. However, Monday morning coincided with very thick fog with some frost and ice. This interfered slightly with a few point operations, etc, thus adding to the difficulties for both drivers and signalmen unaccustomed to the new equipment. There were some delays which were cleared up by noon, and the evening rush hour passed with virtually no delays whatsoever. The associated LNWR lines in and around Exchange station and its approaches were dealt with during the following weekend of 16/17 March. The work was completed satisfactorily and again the Sunday passed without incident. Monday morning brought some fog again but there was little delay. Unfortunately the evening rush hour coincided with very dense fog. There were some misunderstandings between drivers and shunters, and to some extent signalmen, all of which led to delays which tended to become cumulative. By the second day all was well and everything passed off without incident.

When I first became interested in accidents I remarked to an old friend, a retired GC signalman, that the L&Y seemed to have had their fair share. His reply was 'that is only what I would have expected'. This was probably the normal reaction of a railwayman of those days towards rival companies. Nevertheless, Manchester Victoria had its share of misfortune. On 18 August 1925, shortly after 2.00pm, a train from Royton arrived at a suburban platform, the driver failed to bring the train to a stand and ran into the stop block. Many of the passengers were preparing to alight and were

Above:
Hughes '3F' Superheater 0-6-0 No 12537 at Platform 14 at Victoria during 1935. Note that the Belpaire firebox necessitated alteration to the cab 'spectacles'. On some later rebuilds they extended inwards at the top edge (see previous photograph). *W. Potter*

rising from their seats, and a number complained of injuries and shock. The injured were quickly taken to a waiting room where they were given attention by station Ambulance Staff, and it was deemed advisable to convey six passengers including a married couple to hospital. Surprisingly there was no damage to the engine, the vehicles all remained on the rails and the only damage to the train was one broken window. It was suggested that the abnormally heavy load of the train caused the driver's error of judgement.

On 30 July 1926 a foreman platelayer and his mate were run down and killed by a Blackpool express. The tragedy took place near the Pendleton New station about 2½ miles west of Victoria.

An alert signalman at Windsor Bridge Junction watched the 9.40am Liverpool to Leeds express go by on 1 November 1927 and noticed flames and smoke issuing from the last van. He signalled the next box where the train was stopped and the flames extinguished. The train then ran the last mile into Victoria arriving only 10min late. The van was detached before the train was allowed to proceed to Leeds. At Newton Heath two miles east on 26 January 1929 a goods train became derailed; there were no casualties but considerable delays were caused.

Below:
Languishing at Newton Heath in April 1939 is Aspinall radial tank tank No 10733 (Bolton 26C). 'Dreadnought' No 10432 is behind, and a 'Baby Scot' in the background. *W. Potter*

April 1932 unfortunately brought the death of two railwaymen in separate incidents. About 8.45pm on 11 April Driver Harry Hall drew a train of empty stock, mostly luggage and mail vans, eastwards out of the station on to Miles Platting Bank. Travelling on the down south line he was stopped at Millgate home signal. Hall said later that he drew right up to the signal and could not proceed further. Back from the signal there was a track circuit actuating a 'train-waiting' indicator in Millgate box and although this was repeated in Victoria East Junction box it performed no interlocking there. Moreover, it ended 67ft short of the tail of the stationary train. Signalman Higginson in East Junction box was aware of the stationary train, indeed he admitted he could see the tail lamp. Unfortunately he completely misjudged its position, thinking it to be well clear of the up slow line off the loop. Under this mistaken impression he accepted out of Red Bank sidings the empty stock for the 9.00pm Southport departure. He allowed this second empty stock train to proceed down and around the curve into the station. Driver E. Baines said he left Red Bank sidings at 8.30pm and was travelling only very slowly around the severe right-hand curve into the station at a speed of probably not more than 5mph, when he collided with the rear van of a stationary train; the van was simply turned over on to its side. So far as I have been able to discover, Baines was driving a 'Crab'. He said that owing to the severe curvature he was unable to see the stationary train, but his fireman Fred Hammel was keeping a sharp look out. Suddenly Hammel shouted 'Stop!' Later Hammel said 'In the dark I just did not see the train until it was on top of us'. Both enginemen were injured and the guard of the stationary train, T. Tingle of Tonge Road, Leeds, was killed. Signalman Higginson frankly admitted his error and was unable to offer any explanation to account for it. He offered the Leeds empties out of Platform 12 at 8.30pm and they passed him at 8.41pm. He was aware that the train had stopped and he could make out the crossing from his box and thought it was clear. He therefore accepted the Southport empties at 8.42pm. Lt-Col Anderson, reporting on the accident, considered there was a lot of pressure on the signalman. Between 8.00pm and 9.00pm there were 41 train movements to be dealt with. The error of judgement was due to the angle at which the tail lamp was viewed in the dark. He recommended the installation of some mechanical aid to assist the signalmen in the dark. The company officers gave Higginson a very good character. In the past he had been commended on no fewer than three occasions for good and prompt action in averting accidents. He had 41 years service, 18 of them in East Junction box.

Two days later at 7.00am Shunter James A. Davenport of Moston, Manchester was riding in the leading van of an empty train which was being propelled into suburban Platform 10 when he met his death. The Stationmaster reported 'No one saw what happened, all we know is that in some way or other he was caught between the platform and the running board and crushed to death. The only other persons about at the time were the driver and fireman on the engine at the other end of the train'.

On 1 May 1934 two electric trains on the Bury line collided just outside the station. The only casualty was a Mr J. W. Reavet, the Chief Assistant Clerk of Salford Police Court. Mr Reavet was cut about the head by flying glass.

Below:
Leaving Bolton shed in June 1936, a Radial 2-4-2T reboilered by Hughes, No 10693. *W. Potter*

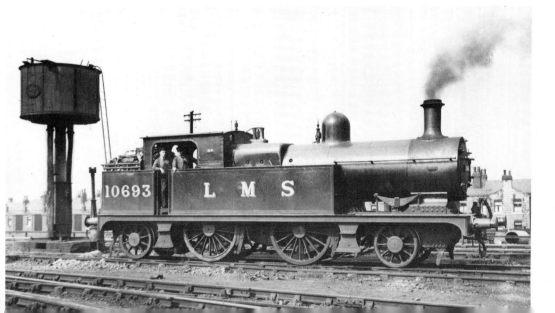

On pilot duty at Victoria in May 1935 is Hughes Radial rebuild No 10835.   *W. Potter*

Empty coaches which had formed the train from Windermere due in at 10.05am on 18 September 1936 were standing at Platform 16 when a train from Southport ran into the rear. Platform 16 was on a most severe right-hand curve and the driver of the Southport train had a 'Black Five' with left-hand drive and would have had a very restricted view of any obstruction at the platform. He realised something was amiss and braked hard, but was unable to stop in time. The 'Black Five' was embedded in the brake van of the train. Guard G. Edwards was inside the van having just taken over from Guard Gordon who had come in with the train. The latter was able to shout a warning to Edwards who then leapt from the van just before the collision. Two months later in thick fog a train arriving from Colne ran into the rear of a second train standing at the platform. One passenger complained of shock but did not require treatment.

When I considered the long steep descent from Miles Platting to Victoria I had the feeling that sooner or later it was inevitable that a loose-coupled goods train would run away, and so it came to pass on New Year's Day 1936. The 8.35am mineral train from Ashton Moss to Aintree, consisting of 42 wagons of slack and a brake van, with an estimated weight of approximately 847 tons, and a total length 310 yards, passed Miles Platting soon after 9.30am drawn by ex-L&Y '6F' 0-8-0 No 12771. At Collyhurst Street signalbox the train was crossed over to the up 'North' line. Adjacent to the signals protecting the cross-over were boards warning drivers of loose-coupled trains to stop and pin down brakes. Driver A. Carter on No 12771 had 23 years service, including eight as a driver. He said at the enquiry that he interpreted the 'STOP' instructions as allowing him a certain amount of discretion, and had on occasions drawn forward to Collyhurst Street box in order that the rear of his train was clear of Miles Platting Junction. He admitted that sometimes with a light train he had gone through without stopping. On this occasion, with a heavy train and a greasy rail to contend with he had intended stopping at the board. He knew the type of engine well, the engine brake was operating satisfactorily and the limit laid down for the class of engine was 44 loaded wagons. Passing Miles Platting station at about 8 to 10mph with steam off and a partial brake application, he almost at once felt the train 'pushing slightly'. He told the fireman, W. H. Hollins, to apply the hand brake. When close to the 'STOP' board he realised the train was not stopping and made a full brake application and applied sand, but with little effect, so when about 15 to 20 wagon lengths beyond the board he told his fireman to get off the engine and endeavour to pin down some wagon brakes.

According to Carter, Hollins alighted without difficulty, taking a brake stick with him, the speed of the train at this point being about 4 to 5mph.

Hollins did not rejoin the engine and Carter then realised that the train was out of control and began to 'pop' on his whistle. As he passed Newtown No 2 box he endeavoured to attract the attention of the signalman by shouting he was running away and at the same time a driver in the nearby sidings also 'popped' his whistle. The signalman came to the window and seemed to rush away again. Carter kept the brake fully applied and thought the wheels first started to skid passing Collyhurst Street box and continued to skid most of the way down the bank.

Guard A. Dickson said that, in accordance with his usual practice, he reminded the driver before leaving Ashton Moss to stop at Miles Platting to pin down brakes. The train was brought almost to a stand at Ashton Branch Sidings box, about a quarter of a mile before Miles Platting. He confirmed Driver Carter's estimate of speed (10mph) through Miles Platting station, where he applied his hand brake as usual to assist the driver to stop at the board. He did not screw the brake down fully until passing the trailing junction as he had not up to this time anticipated any difficulty in stopping at the board. He first felt concern when the train did not stop at or a few wagons beyond the board. He became further alarmed when speed began to increase and his van wheels commenced to skid, he released his brakes and reapplied, after which there seemed to be no further skidding. He was well acquainted with the regulation but he said trains stopped beyond the board more often than at it. He thought they passed the board at 10mph.

There were two signalmen in Collyhurst Street box. J. E. Sykes in charge and F. Jones. Sykes said the signals were off for the train which passed at about 4 to 5mph. Sykes saw the fireman get off the engine and run alongside the train, although the train did not stop and the fireman was unable to rejoin the engine he did not realise there was anything wrong or that the train was running away. He heard no whistle until a few minutes after the train had passed. He added he had often seen unfitted trains run by without stopping, but not as heavy as this. He knew this was wrong but had not drawn attention to it. Signalman Jones who attended to goods line only was not exceptionally busy when the train was passing. He noticed it did not stop to pin down brakes, but this did not cause him any concern, as he had on occasion seen quite heavy trains pass without stopping. Moreover the train passed at walking pace and he booked 4min for it to clear the section, about 700yd to Newton No 2 box. He did not see the fireman on the line. Both signalmen said it was quite usual for trains to draw well forward of the board before stopping.

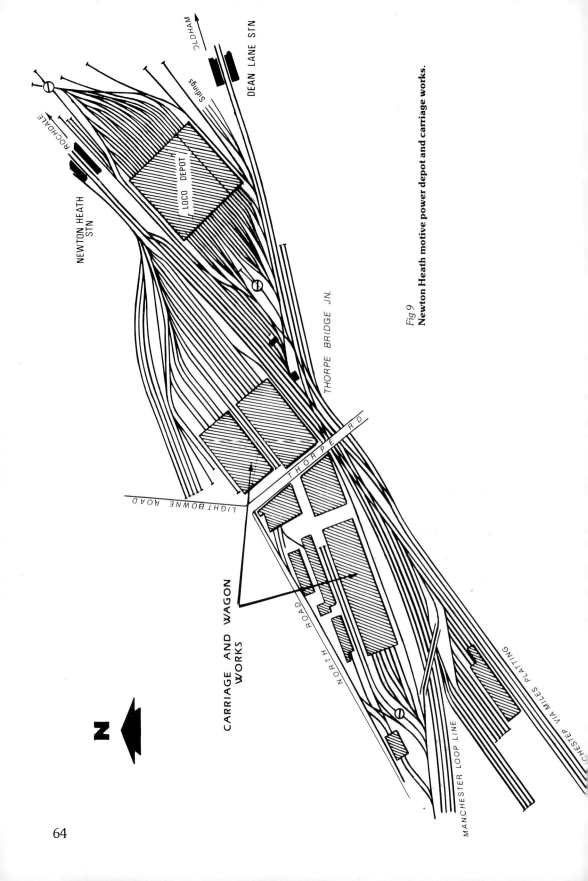

OLDHAM

DEAN LANE STN

Sidings

ROCHDALE

NEWTON HEATH STN

LOCO DEPOT

THORPE BRIDGE JN.

LIGHTBOWNE ROAD

THORPE RD

CARRIAGE AND WAGON WORKS

NORTH ROAD

MANCHESTER LOOP LINE

CHESTER VIA MILES PLATTING

N

Fig 9
Newton Heath motive power depot and carriage works.

64

Signalman I. Firth at Newton No 2 had the road clear for the train and said that just before reaching his box he heard the whistle 'popping' and the driver shouted something as he passed. Having previously heard drivers whistle for the guard's brake Firth concluded the guard's brake was wanted on this occasion. Not realising the train was out of control, he took no action beyond shouting to the guard to put on his brake. This seems rather strange in view of the fact that Firth went on to say that sparks were flying from the wheels of the brake van. He also said that although the train was travelling rather quickly he had seen goods trains go by as fast on other occasions. He did not notice there was only one man on the footplate. He thought the speed was about 20mph.

At Newtown No 1 box there were two signalmen, T. H. Shaw and W. H. Winrow. Both realised at once that the train was running away, from the unusual speed at which it passed. They thought about 35mph. It passed under clear signals (except for the fixed distant) at 9.46am, at which time Winrow sent 'Train entering section' to Millgate box, followed at once by 'Train running away on right road'. Shaw noticed there was only one man on the footplate and that the engine wheels were skidding, but that the van wheels were revolving.

T. Speed, one of two signalmen at Millgate box passed forward the 'Train running away on right road' signal to Victoria East Junction box as soon as he received it, and the train passed almost at the same time. He thought the speed was about 60mph, and that the engine wheels were skidding. He also telephoned Victoria East Junction that the train was travelling very fast.

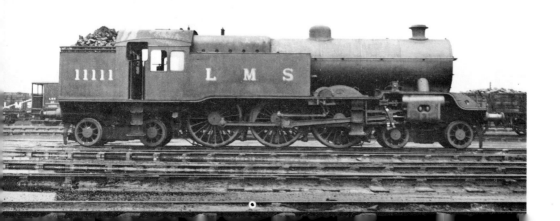

At Victoria East Signalmen A. C. Nicholson and A. Sharpley had very little time to decide the best course of action and to safeguard other impending train movements. There was not a clear road available and it was decided the best that could be done in the circumstances was to put the run-away into Platform 14. Standing at the west end of the platform were three non-corridor bogies which were to form the 9.54am all stations to Preston. The engine had not yet been attached, a fact which was also taken into account. The three coaches had been built in 1907 and 1910 and their total weight was only 76 tons. The collision was violent, No 12771 penetrating 8ft 6in into the brake compartment of the rear coach. The body of this vehicle and the middle vehicle were telescoped to the extent of 6ft. The whole being propelled forward over 300yd after impact, before coming to a stand. The now adverse gradient helping somewhat no doubt. Guard James H. Hayes of Blackpool was in the van sorting parcels when the collision took place. He was found unconscious beneath a heap of parcels, indeed it was suggested the volume of parcels may well have saved his life. The leading coach had all windows shattered, splintered woodwork and deranged seats. Fortunately only nine passengers were aboard the train,

eight of whom, including four railwaymen, were only slightly injured. Along with the guard they were taken to hospital for treatment.

Major G. R. S. Wilson conducted the enquiry and obviously concluded that the accident was caused by the failure to stop and pin down brakes and that Driver Carter had failed to make the prescribed stop and must be held primarily responsible. However, although not raining, the weather was damp and misty and Major Wilson accepted Carter's account and considered that he was guilty only of mismanagement of his brake and misjudgement. However, his handling of the brake must call for criticism, as he failed to apply full brake or use sand until almost at the board. Also if he had released and reapplied the brake from time-to-time during the descent of the bank, the brake would probably have had better effect and although he could hardly have regained control of the train, the speed at the foot of the incline might well have been appreciably lessened. It was also difficult to understand why he had not told his fireman to get off the engine as soon as he realised the full brake application had not been effective. The signalmen at Collyhurst Street and Newtown No 2 also bore some measure of responsibility. On the other hand all other signalmen involved carried out their duties with credit, especially so at Victoria East. It seemed likely that the estimated speeds of the train were exaggerated. Signalbox timings indicate an average speed of 12 to 15mph and it is unlikely that the ultimate speed exceeded 25 to 30mph. The damage to the passenger train would appear consistent with this estimate.

Probably because it was New Year's Day, treated as a holiday in Manchester long before it became a public holiday, newspaper reports were nothing like as comprehensive as I would have expected and I have not traced any pictures. One report said it had been revealed that the drivers of goods trains did not usually bother to stop and pin down brakes if the load was less than 40 wagons. It was also stated that despite the long severe down gradient this was believed to be the first instance of a run-away.

Fireman Hollins was unable to attend the enquiry on account of a serious illness (nothing to do with the accident). He submitted a written statement. In the statement he confirmed that Driver Carter had intended stopping at the board. He said that after alighting from the engine he had succeeded in dropping eight or nine wagon brakes as they passed him, but had been unable to pin them down. He did not think of informing the signalman at Collyhurst Street what had occurred. For myself I find what happened to Hollins next rather curious. Did he continue down the bank on foot? Or perhaps he thumbed a lift?

No 12771 was not derailed and suffered comparatively little damage, mainly at the leading end. Of the mineral train, the 25th, 26th, 28th and 30th wagons suffered varying degrees of damage. The derailment of the 25th wagon considerably damaged the permanent way, 277 chairs and 18 sleepers being broken. The brake van of the mineral train was slightly damaged. Stationmaster's clerk J. Lennon telephoned for ambulances as soon as he heard the sound of the collision.

The first, maybe, but not the last runaway, the LMS era was to end with another great and spectacular drama. For this we move forward to the early hours of 11 December 1947. Driver G. Brewin and Fireman L. Hopper, both of Patricroft, were aboard a Western section train en route from Neville Hill, Leeds, to Eccles. In normal course they would travel the through road at Victoria crossing over to the LNWR at Exchange. They had ex-LNWR 0-8-0 rebuild, No 8903, and a load of petrol behind the tender. At about 3.30am the train was standing at Collyhurst Street signals. The signal presumably was at danger, because it becomes evident that Brewin had no intention of stopping to pin down brakes. In any case a goods train had only recently gone through. Brewin's train was made up of a front runner wagon, 20 full tanker wagons, a rear runner wagon and 20-ton brake van. The weight of No 8903, her tender and remaining coal and water was estimated at 92ton 15cwt, the total weight of the train at about 593 tons and the total train length over buffers at 527ft. The weather was very damp with patchy fog. It was suggested on Brewin's behalf that as the weather was fine and clear at Leeds he may not have realised how bad the weather was going down the bank. From my own experiences I would have expected the weather to have been deteriorating from leaving the tunnel at Diggle if there was fog about. A goods train from Ashton Moss had preceded the arrival of No 8903 at Collyhurst Street and it may well be that the latter had to stand for several minutes. The guard alighted and pinned down the brakes on the rear runner wagon: regulations prohibited the

Right:
'Pugs' Nos 11207 and 11234 resting at Newton Heath in April 1939. One would find these midgets trundling around Salford yard, for which task their 3ft driving wheels made them very well suited. *W. Potter*

Below right:
Aspinall rebuilt large numbers of Barton Wright 0-6-0 tender engines as 0-6-0STs. Pictured here is No 11336 of Bank Hall (23A), seen ex-works on Bolton shed in August 1937. *W. Potter*

pinning down of brakes of petrol tankers. Fireman Hopper would have pinned down the brakes of the leading runner wagon but alleged he was prevented from doing so by his driver who said it would not be necessary. It was also stated that Driver Brewin refused the assistance of a second engine which was available at the top of the bank to provide extra braking power if needed. It was said that Brewin maintained that No 8903 was a very fine engine which was well able to manage the train. In fact when he knew he was rostered for this particular train he had specially asked if he might have this engine. In due course the Collyhurst Street signalman pulled off for the up 'South' road and Brewin released his brakes. Immediately the train began to move forward, speed increased rapidly and a brake application only succeeded in locking the wheels. Brewin next wound his gear into reverse and opened his regulator, the driving

wheels spun furiously but the speed of the train continued to increase. Those of us who remember these engines can imagine the scene; almost certainly oozing steam from every possible outlet, probably making loud shrill noises reminiscent of a stuck pig, the exhaust and spinning wheels creating the most fearful racket, No 8903 must have presented the most fearsome sight viewed through the fog. Brewin closed the regulator and reapplied the brake. No 8903 continued to career downhill through the murky blackness. On account of the fog, steam and darkness, Fireman Hopper could not see whether the brakes were effective or the sanders working. He made a hazardous trip out on to the running plate of the engine, where he found the brakes locked and could smell hot sand and see sparks flying from the wheels.

Newton No 2 box was closed for the night. Signalman Ballantine in Newtown No 1 heard the

Above:
Three types of L&Y 0-8-0 resting at the rear of Newton Heath shed in about 1934. (Left to right) Hughes unsuperheated '6F' No 12827, Aspinall unsuperheated '5F' No 12741 and Hughes '7F' superheater rebuild No 12971. *W. Potter*

Below:
As yet unnamed, 'Jubilee' No 5650 is seen passing Victoria East Junction signalbox at the foot of Miles Platting Bank with a train for Manchester Exchange in May 1936. *W. Potter*

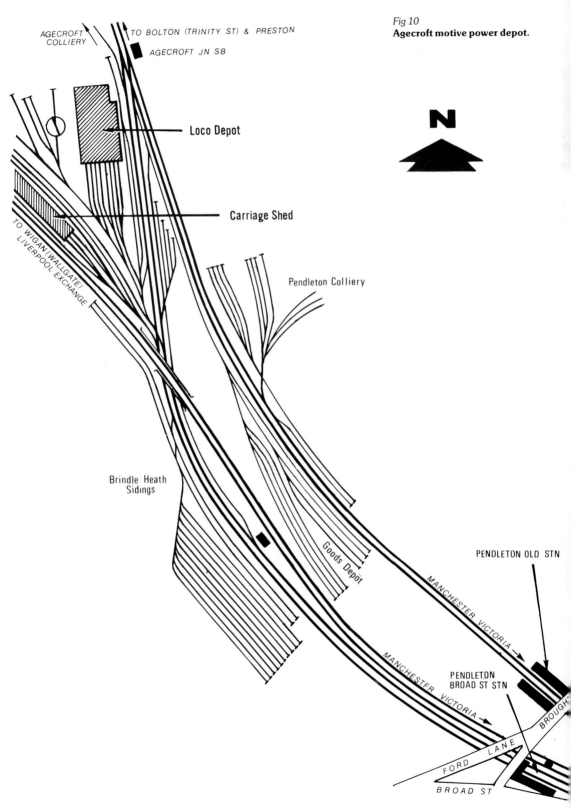

AGECROFT
COLLIERY

TO BOLTON (TRINITY ST) & PRESTON

AGECROFT JN SB

Loco Depot

Carriage Shed

TO WIGAN (WALLGATE)
LIVERPOOL EXCHANGE

Pendleton Colliery

Brindle Heath
Sidings

Goods Depot

MANCHESTER VICTORIA →

MANCHESTER VICTORIA →

PENDLETON OLD STN

PENDLETON
BROAD ST STN

BROUGH

FORD LANE

BROAD ST

Fig 10
Agecroft motive power depot.

N

Above:
Standing on a through road at Victoria in May 1936 is 'Crab' No 2822, one of the five fitted with Lentz rotary cam poppet valve gear. *W. Potter*

runaway signal from No 8903 at 3.48am, 1min before she clattered past his box. He immediately sent 'Train running away on right road' to Signalman Shaw at Millgate box. This prompt action enabled Shaw to notify Signalman Jones at Turntable box that the runaway would have to be diverted into a suburban platform road, the through road being occupied by the Ashton Moss goods which had quite properly stopped to unpin brakes. Jones routed the runway into Platform 7 which was unoccupied. No 8903 was estimated to be travelling at 25mph as she approached the buffers; she over-rode the buffers, ran across the concourse and finally came to rest just short of the booking office windows. On her way she had very fortuitously run straight between two pillars supporting the roof and part of the administration offices.

Remarkably No 8903 suffered little damage with only a buffer beam buckled and brake gear, sand pipes and rail guards broken or damaged. She was eventually towed away on her own wheels. The leading runner wagon was completely demolished and the three leading tankers were derailed with underframes buckled and the tanks strained and leaking. The 10th vehicle, the rear runner wagon and the brake van were undamaged. The remainder suffered only minor damage, the 15th and 19th derailed one pair of wheels.

There was of course some concern that leaking petrol might lead to a further catasrophe. The Fire Brigade were quickly on the scene, the area was cleared and the contents of the damaged wagons pumped into road vehicles. A spokesman for Area Control expressed surprise that the tankers contained petrol, as they had believed the vehicles to be empty. Brewin and Hopper were taken to

hospital. Hopper was not seriously injured but Brewin died. He was 48, had 31 years service with the railway, 21 as a fireman and five as a driver.

I can well imagine the progress of No 8903 coming down to Victoria. Many times I recall observing, and hearing a LNWR 0-8-0 rattling along with a goods train at a smart pace. Indeed if I remember correctly there was a well documented instance of one of them achieving 58mph, when pressed into service on an up express at Bletchley in about 1935 or 1936 after the failure of the train engine. Conversely I cannot recall ever seeing an L&Y 0-8-0 travelling at other than a sedate and rather ponderous pace.

To continue the narrative on a more cheerful note a visit to the Newton Heath sheds on the evening of Saturday 25 May 1935 revealed, apart from the usual conglomeration of ex-L&Y tank and goods engines, 14 Fowler 2-6-2Ts, four Fowler 2-6-4Ts, one LMS-built '2P' 4-4-0, three 'Prince of Wales' 4-6-0s; including rather strangely No 25660 *Kestrel* sporting an Oxenholme plate, four LMS-built 'Compounds', seven Hughes 4-6-0s, one 'Baby Scot', three 'Crabs' and three 'Black Fives'. Saturday evening is surely reflected in the number of 2-6-2Ts on shed and the shortage of 'Crabs' indicates some excursion traffic I would suggest.

A revealing and interesting comparison of the changing times can be made by comparing locomotive class totals on two Saturday visits to Victoria, on 19 October 1935 and 22 October 1938 respectively. 'Crabs': 24 and 11, 'Black Fives': 6 and 16, 'Jubilees': 1 and 6, '2Ps' 4-4-0s: 4 and 4, 'Compounds': 9 and 6, Hughes 4-6-0s: 8 and 3, 'Baby Scots': 0 and 2 and 'Prince of Wales' 4-6-0s: 4 and 0. There was the usual cluster of L&Y 0-6-0s on banking and station duties on both occasions. Also the expected variety of tank engines from the little 'Radials' up to the huge Baltics, and on the second visit these included one Stanier 2-6-2T and nine Stanier 2-6-4Ts. A couple of the latter may have been on jobs worked by 'Crabs' on the earlier

Above:
Stanier 2-6-0 No 42975 ex-Horwich Works, standing on Bolton Shed on 5 August 1960. The locomotive is carrying a 3D shedplate. *W. Potter*

occasion. Also on the second visit 'Jinty' No 7509 was included among those on banking duty.

The Victoria scene would not be complete without some mention of the Bury services. There was a choice of route. The main commuter service over a steeply graded line via Prestwich and Whitefield had been converted to third rail electric traction some seven years prior to grouping and afforded trains in either direction at 20min intervals on weekdays. This service was strengthened during the rush hour periods. On Sundays there was a half-hour service. Calling at six intermediate stations the outward trip took 24min terminating at Bolton Street station. The inward trip was scheduled for a 22min duration. For confirmed steam addicts there were alternatives. An infrequent service ran via Newton Heath and Heywood to Bury Knowsley Street, in many instances involving changing trains at Castleton. An even less frequent service left Victoria in the opposite direction from a main line

platform and travelled via Clifton Junction and Radcliffe Bridge to Bury Bolton Street, several of the rush hour trains commencing or terminating at Salford.

By the time World War 2 was upon us Stanier locomotives were well entrenched on the old Central Division with the mixed traffic types still dominating the scene. Among the 'Jubilees' it was noticeable that Polmadie were frequently using one on their Manchester turns. As indicated earlier Blackpool remained loyal to the 'Dreadnoughts' although 'Compounds' were more frequent and the occasional 'Jubilee' might appear. 'Compounds' continued to be daily visitors from Southport and Low Moor. On the local scene there had been a further increase in the number of Stanier tank engines. The six remaining Baltics were at Agecroft and continued to play their part until their relatively early demise.

Below:
The last of the Hughes rail motors No 10617 at Bolton Trinity Street Station in May 1938. It was the only one of its type to last until 1948. *W. Potter*

4 Central
The Cheshire Lines Committee and the Wigan Branch

The Cheshire Lines Committee, jointly administered by the Manchester, Sheffield and Lincoln, the Great Northern and the Midland Railway in the first instance, and subsequently by the LNER and LMS, had their own rolling stock but no locomotives. These were provided by courtesy of the MS&L, GC and LNER in that order. The station was opened in 1880 replacing a temporary one which became the goods yard. Inside the building one appreciated the superb arched glass roof, a single span of 210ft rising to a height of 90ft above rail level. The impression was of considerably more light and air than was usually associated with a railway station during the days of steam. Alas there was a blot on the picture. The frontage, booking offices and some of the general offices, were wooden structures. In the first place announced to be temporary, they were still in use some 90 years later when the station finally closed. Underneath the cover of the roof were Platforms 1 to 6. Outside the wall supporting the roof, on the left as one entered the station was Platform 8. There was a short bay, Platform 7, between Platforms 6 and 8, and shortly after the opening a wooden Platform 9 was also erected. Between each pair of platform roads was a

centre road enabling an engine to run round the train if required. These centre roads were known as A, B, C, and D roads. In February 1936 a 170-ton turntable was installed, which was converted to vacuum operation in January 1937. The last mile and a half or so of the approach to the terminus was on viaducts, originally built to carry two roads. The viaducts were later widened, and in some places separate viaducts constructed alongside the originals, to accommodate five roads. The left-hand tracks leaving the station were known as 'A route', the right-hand (Liverpool) tracks as 'B route' and the other line as 'centre road'. An unusual situation arose where the Midland and GC line trains joined the CLC at Throstle Nest East Junction. The CLC up line ran into Manchester, thus trains coming in on the down line from the Midland and the GC,

Below:
'J69' No 7363 at Gorton in 1935. These diminutive tank engines were part of the daily scene at Manchester Central station and Deansgate goods yards during the 1930s. *W. Potter*

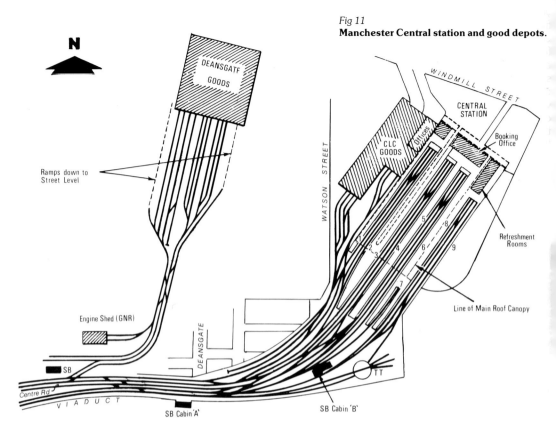

Fig 11
Manchester Central station and good depots.

N

DEANSGATE GOODS

CENTRAL STATION

WINDMILL STREET

Booking Office

CLC GOODS

Offices

Ramps down to Street Level

WATSON STREET

Refreshment Rooms

Engine Shed (GNR)

DEANSGATE

Line of Main Roof Canopy

SB

TT

Centre Rd

VIADUCT

SB Cabin 'A'

SB Cabin 'B'

suddenly found themselves on the up line. The loop from Fairfield to Central via Fallowfield was opened to Fallowfield in 1891 and throughout in 1892. The approach road must have been under considerable pressure by this time, the widening not being completed until 1893. On completion the centre road was intended for shunting purposes and for stabling empty coaching stock. Staff were urged to exercise the greatest care to ensure such stock was properly secured before being left unattended on this line as there was a falling gradient of 1 in 100 towards Cornbrook. The centre road was not to be used as a through line except under 'Single Line working' regulations with the supervision of a pilotman. During foggy weather or falling snow, or during the hours of darkness, vehicles left standing on the centre road were to show a white light attached to the rear vehicle. In foggy weather a detonator was to be placed not less than 50yd from the end of such vehicles.

Once trains had commenced running to Fallowfield the portion of line between Chorlton Junction and Manchester Central was transferred from the jurisdiction of the Midland to the CLC.

The terminus was nominally a CLC building but all interested parties ran trains into the station, the GN exercising running powers over the GC. The

GN also built a splendidly enormous double-deck goods yard and warehouse at Deansgate, adjacent to Central, access to which was via a short branch which diverged from the main line at a point about 30 chains from the terminus known as GN Junction. The branch ran into the upper deck of 10 roads, and two further roads (one either side) dropped steeply to the lower deck. The diminutive tank engines employed in the yards were expected to haul six loaded wagons up these ramps.

There was always plenty of activity and a great variety of engines, coaching stock and goods vehicles to be found in the station and yards.

Between the Grouping in 1923 and Nationalisation in 1948 the LNER provided motive power for the CLC and by and large an existing practice was continued. That is to say almost 100% of the locomotives provided were of Great Central origin. The only exceptions which spring readily to mind were a few 'J39' 0-6-0s and the odd 'K3' 2-6-0, although soon after the Grouping there was a large GN Atlantic at Liverpool for a short while, and during the early 1930s a few ex-Great Northern 'D2' 4-4-0s made an appearance, as did some rather similar looking 4-4-2T locomotives towards the end of the 1930s. The GN maintained a small stud of the 'J6' 0-6-0s at Trafford Park for some years to work their goods trains to Colwick and at first a stud of 'J52' tanks to work Deansgate goods yard. After a few years the LNER replaced the former with ex-GC 'B9' 4-6-0s and the latter with ex-Great Eastern 'J69' tank engines. Generally speaking one could have been forgiven for concluding that the engines allocated to the CLC were ones for which the parent company considered they themselves had no further use. In the early days after grouping one might see a Pollit 'Single' with 7ft 9in driving wheels, or the last

Parker double-framed 4-4-0 working out of Southport, until her withdrawal in 1926. 'D5' 4-4-0 locomotives also worked from Southport until 1928, after which they moved to Trafford Park and then were steadily withdrawn, the last — No 5699 — going in March 1933. In their final days they might occasionally be found working a Guide Bridge local along the Fallowfield line. Nevertheless some of these old engines served the CLC very well and in many instances for very long periods of time. None more so than the Pollit 'D6' 4-4-0s. At

Above:
Parker 'D5' 4-4-0 No 5695 at Gorton in early livery in the late 1920s. *Great Central Railway Society Collection*

Left:
A Trafford Park favourite Pollitt 'D6' 4-4-0 No 5856 departing from Platfrom 2 at Central with a Liverpool express in June 1937. No 5856 was at Trafford at the Grouping, remaining until February 1938. *W. Potter*

Grouping all 33 of the class were on the line, four of which — Nos 5857/59/69/76 — were Westinghouse Brake fitted. No 5857 retained this equipment until withdrawal in 1931, the equipment being removed from the other three during the early 1930s. Always referred to locally simply as 'Pollits' these engines worked the Liverpool 'Flyers', with a booked journey time of 45min with a stop at Warrington; certain trains were booked for a 40min non-stop journey. The first withdrawal took place during 1930 — No 5873 of Liverpool. No 5866, a Trafford Park engine until moving to Southport in 1928, also made her last journey to Gorton during that year. Six more Trafford engines followed during 1931, and a further eight by the end of 1933. Two years elapsed before the next withdrawal after which they disappeared in ones and twos until at the outbreak of war there were only nine remaining. No doubt these would soon have followed had not the war intervened. No 5869 and 5879 were withdrawn during 1943 having spent their entire LNER time at Liverpool. The remainder saw out the war but none completed the LNER era. Nos 5874 and 5880 moved to Lincoln in May 1937 at which time they are believed to have been languishing at Gorton after recent visits to the works. The former returned to the CLC after three years but the latter was broken up during 1939. No 5856, one of the class behind which I have memories of a very fast run on a Liverpool train, also moved to Lincoln in

1938 in a swap for 'D9' No 6036. No 5856 was scrapped less than a year later and replaced by No 5865, the latter however returned to the CLC after 12 months. Many express locomotives spent most of their lives on far more glamorous duties, but I would suggest that few were more regular revenue earners than these gallant little engines. Many will recall the time when a visit to Central, even if only for a few minutes, ensured the sight of one or two of the class. Northwich, about mid-way along the line to Chester, had during the 1920s half-a-dozen Parker 'D7' 4-4-0s — a few years older than the 'D6s' but very similar in appearance. After these were moved away during the summer of 1930 the shed was without any passenger tender locomotives until towards the end of 1941 when 'D6' No 5865 arrived. Nos 5855 and 5874 ended their days at Northwich being the last withdrawals in December 1947.

It was I think almost inevitable that as the 'D6' numbers declined they would be replaced by the larger but by no means dissimilar 'D9s' followed by the 'D10s' and ultimately the 'D11s' all of which were Robinson-built engines. So it was at Northwich, first with 'D9s' Nos 6018 and 6038 then 'D10s' Nos 5429/31/34. In fact No 5436 was the first 'D10' at Northwich but she stayed only a matter of weeks. During the 1930s the passenger engines at Northwich were 'C13' 4-4-2Ts (the usual quota was five) assisted in their work from time to time by 'J10' 0-6-0s and 'N5' 0-6-2Ts.

In fact there had been a 'D9' at Liverpool in the 1920s for the working of the Hull train, followed by the 'C1' mentioned earlier. In the late 1920s the working of the Hull trains was transferred to Neepsend, Sheffield. The first 'D9' to arrive on the scene for CLC service was No 5104 *Queen Alexandra* posted to Brunswick, Liverpool in May

Below:
Ivatt 'D2' 4-4-0 No 4381 at Platform 8 in June 1935.
W. Potter

Above:
Robinson's 'D9' engines soon established themselves on the CLC as they replaced the 'D6s'. Brunswick's No 6020 is seen after arriving at Central with an express from Liverpool in June 1937. *W. Potter*

1933. In fact over two years were to elapse before a further four arrived. Meanwhile a number of Liverpool trains were worked by the Neepsend Atlantics as part of a diagram which brought the engine from Sheffield to Manchester, Manchester to Liverpool, and Liverpool to Sheffield via Stockport Tiviot Dale and Godley Junction, or in the reverse direction around the triangle. In December 1936

more radical changes took place. Some of the Gorton diagrams were reshaped to include a certain amount of working over the CLC. Among the more noteworthy was that which involved an engine running light to Godley Junction to pick up and convey the mail to Liverpool via Tiviot Dale, thence to Manchester arriving at 8.23am, and after turning, forward with the 9.25am up Hull. The engine which brought the local down from Fairfield, arriving at 8.40am, which had formerly worked the Hull train, spent the day on Liverpool trains. A further

Below:
Trafford Park 'J39' No 1295 on shed in June 1934. 'F2' No 5783 is behind. *W. Potter*

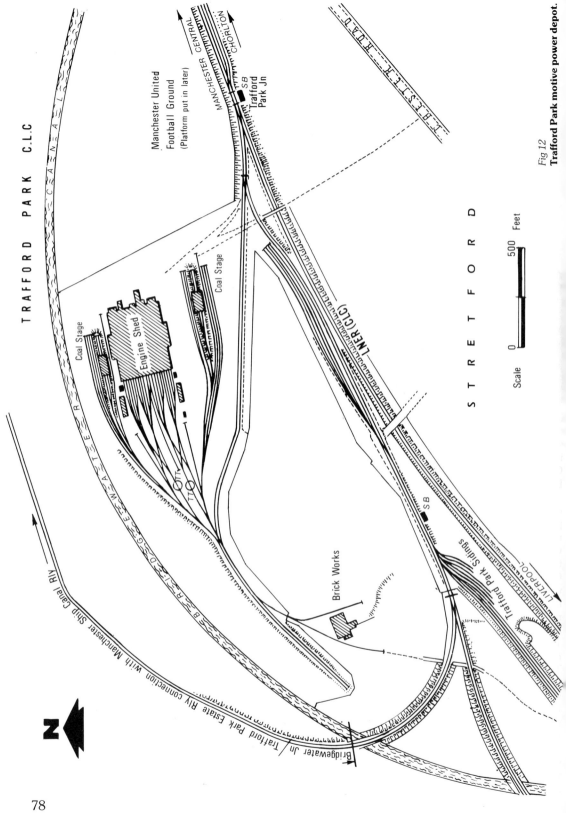

TRAFFORD PARK C.L.C

Manchester United
Football Ground
(Platform put in later)

MANCHESTER CENTRAL

CHORLTON

S B
Trafford
Park Jn

Coal Stage

Engine Shed

Coal Stage

LNER (CLC)

STRETFORD

TRA FFORD

Brick Works

Trafford Park Sidings

S B

LIVERPOOL

CANAL

R I V E R   M E R S E Y

B R I D G E W A T E R

Bridgewater Jn   Trafford Park Estate Rly connection with Manchester Ship Canal

Manchester Ship Canal Rly

N

Scale

0   500   Feet

Fig 12
Trafford Park motive power depot.

Above:
Chester 'C13' No 7413 (formerly 5178) passing Brooklands in August 1947. *W. Potter*

innovation saw the engine which arrived with the train from Leicester at 11.16am take the 'all stations' service to Guide Bridge at 12.10pm, where it was remanned before running light engine to Central to take charge of the Harwich-Liverpool Boat Train which departed at 2.00pm.

Heaton Mersey depot at Stockport had a couple of passenger diagrams which brought their two passenger engines into Manchester during the morning. During the 1920s their passenger engines were 'C13' 4-4-2Ts, one of the diagrams returning the engine from Manchester to Stockport via Chortlon and the Midland line. I was still very young when we moved and had a house quite near the line, and clearly remember my astonishment one morning when I beheld a bright green tank engine approaching along the Midland line. In the early 1930s the tank engines were replaced by a couple of 'D6s' until the five 'D2' engines arrived at Trafford Park during the winter of 1932/33. These were Nos 4361/78/81/92/99; Nos 4361 and 4381 were despatched forthwith to Heaton Mersey and the Pollits recalled. I do not believe it is any secret the 'D2s' were looked upon as decidedly inferior on the CLC, and the fact that Brunswick never had one tells its own story. It is my belief that after a very short time the ones at Trafford were only rostered to the important diagrams in an emergency. The two at Heaton Mersey remained until April 1934, the

ones at Trafford were pottering about until about July 1935 when three disappeared or were possibly put in store. Nos 4361 and 4392 were sent to Heaton Mersey; the Pollits once more returning to the main line. It is thought that No 4392 was ex-works and No 4361 may well have been in the works as she was late arriving at Heaton Mersey, 'J10' No 5121 standing in. No 5880 was posted to Heaton Mersey around 29 October and No 5270 on 4 November. Meanwhile the performance of the GN engines had been erratic in the extreme, one or both being absent more often that not since 12 September, 'J10' No 5077 standing in assisted by 'D6' No 5878 which had been loaned. The two 'D6s' remained for about 13 and 21 months respectively and were replaced by sister engines, which were in turn so replaced until 1942 when Heaton Mersey received their first two 'D9' locomotives Nos 6016 and 6025. Shortly before this they had been allocated two 'B9' 4-6-0s.

For their own goods traffic the CLC relied on the 'J10s' for most of the LNER era. Trafford Park had four or five of the larger 'J11s' until the mid-1930s

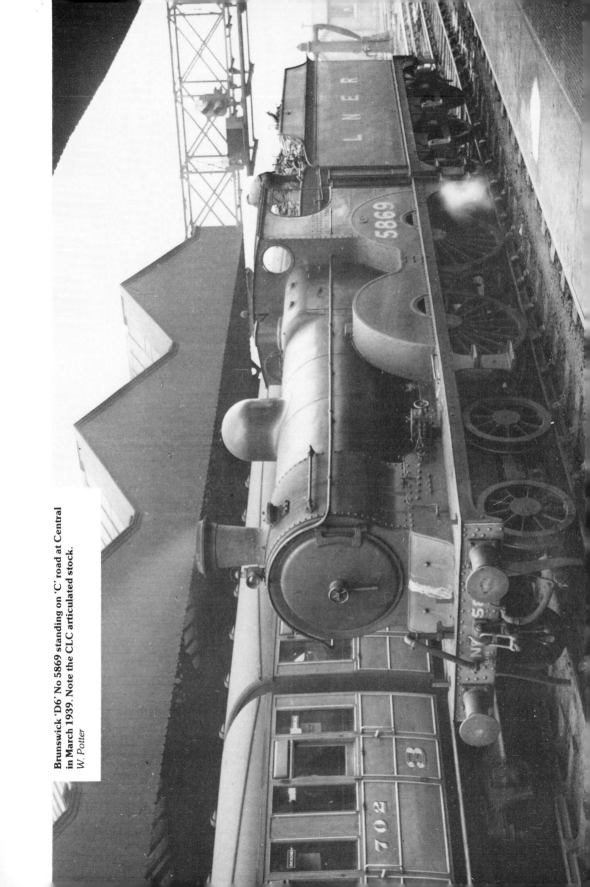

Brunswick 'D6' No 5869 standing on 'C' road at Central in March 1939. Note the CLC articulated stock.
W. Potter

when they were largely replaced by the more modern 'J39s'. However, these larger engines were often used on through trains to the LNER system. When used on the CLC they would often be on stopping passenger trains or excursions to Southport or Haydock Park Races, not forgetting of course Aintree, particularly on Grand National Day. Latterly Trafford Park had a 'K3' 2-6-0 on strength. Goods engines often tended to remain at one shed for longer periods of time than the passenger engines. In this respect Stockport had several 'J10s' for lengthy spells, notably No 5119 from 1911 until after nationalisation. This locomotive was remarkable also for the length of time she remained in pre-1929 livery. The last record I have of her with her number still on the tender being 1938. She could well have been the last engine displaying this style of painting. Trafford Park had a 'J11' running around in similar condition until well into the 1930s, but for nothing like as long as No 5119.

Wigan engines were often to be found in and around Manchester. At the Grouping they had a number of elderly Sacre 0-6-0s which they retained for some years. Indeed I cannot trace a 'J10' to Wigan, the first example being No 5812, until December 1927 when the older engines began to depart for the last time. Subsequently Wigan's sole allocation was often a dozen or so of this class. Occasionally they had an 'N5' and once a 'J11' for a short while. Prior to 1930 they had an 'F1' 2-4-2T for the local service to Lowton St Mary, which was fitted for push-pull working if I am not mistaken. Throughout the 1930s they had a railcar for this service — No 51908 *Expedition* was followed by No 51914 *Royal Forrester* and finally No 51915, the ex-Axholme Joint Line Car which did not have a name. The car was very unpopular and, as one driver once said to me 'the damn thing spends more time at Gorton works than here'. This was probably a bit of an exaggeration, but it is true the car was very frequently at Gorton. The Wigan water supply was supposed to contain a large amount of 'foreign bodies and vegetable matter' which was most unsuitable for the cars but evidently had little effect on the 'J10s'! A 'J10' stood in when the car was absent; after car No 51915 had departed, motor-fitted 'C13' and 'F1' tanks had short spells but I believe the duty was ultimately allocated to the inevitable 'J10'. Before leaving the Wigan district, I must emphasis that strangely enough the Wigan branch and shed did not fall within the jurisdiction of the old CLC, but was in fact an outpost of the old GC. At Lowton St Mary a line diverged over the short distance to St Helens. In LNER days most trains ran to St Helens with the shuttle service between Lowton and Wigan. Timetables suggest that in earlier days the shuttle was between Lowton and St Helens.

The line through Northwich to Chester would seem never to have tried to compete with the LNWR route from Exchange, and there was nothing which could even remotely be described as an express. The Northwich engines have already been mentioned and all I can say about Chester shed is that it usually played host to about five 'C13s', two or three 'N5s' (reduced to one in the 1930s), and a 'J62', all tank engines, and from 1934 onwards a couple of 'J10s'. I cannot trace any passenger tender engines at the shed. At least one of the 'C13' class could usually be seen in Manchester during the day.

Some two miles distant from Central station the Manchester United Football Club had their ground at the side of the Liverpool line. In 1935 a single wooden platform halt was erected on the up side. On match days a shuttle service ran between Central and the ground. The trains were made up of elderly non-corridor coaches hauled variously by 'C13' and 'N5' tanks and 'J10' 0-6-0s. I am not a regular visitor to the ground but the last time I saw the trains in about 1949, a very weary looking 'N5' and 'J10' were in charge.

Station pilot work and much of the empty stock working was performed by 'N5' or 'F1' tanks, exceptions being usually worked by main line engines filling in time. I have heard it said that the tank engine which brought in the empty stock would sometimes lend assistance on departure if the train was heavy, but I never saw such a thing happen myself. Indeed, if the train was a long one the tank would usually run clear via the centre road after which the train engine would propel the vehicles up to the buffer stops.

A little bit of excitement for spotters along the Chester line was afforded by the rather intermittent practice of working an engine ex-works from Gorton on the first stopping train in the morning, returning with what might have been generously described as a 'semi-fast' which arrived back in Manchester at around 10.45am. I witnessed many rare and resplendent machines returning light to Gorton after their exertions, and indeed on occasion used to rise early to watch them running down having had prior notice from a signalman friend at the Wilbraham Road box.

Happily comparatively few accidents would seem to have occurred, certainly of sufficient interest to attract the local press. On 15 November 1923, at a location 9½ miles out along the Liverpool line, a mineral train ran into the rear of a stationary goods train. Several wagons from both trains were derailed, some of which were demolished. There were no casualties but services in both directions were delayed for some hours. Five years later on 9 November 1928 in dense fog, the 10.00am stopping train from St Helens Central ran into the rear of a stationary goods train near Trafford Park.

Top:
'J62' 0-6-0ST No 5893 on Trafford Park shed in June 1934. The 12 engines of this class spent most of their lives in the Wrexham, Bidston and Chester areas. *W. Potter*

Above:
'J62' 0-6-0T No 5277, recently ex-shops, is seen here at Trafford Park in July 1935. The seven engines of the class spent most of their lives in and around Immingham, although one or two made occasional sorties into North Wales. *W. Potter*

Top right:
Brunswick 'F2' 2-4-2T No 5783 at Trafford Park in June 1934. *W. Potter*

Bottom right:
Inside Trafford Park shed in June 1933. Visible are 'C13s' Nos 5199 and 5454, 'J69' No 7273 and 'D2' No 4399. *W. Potter*

Several passengers were cut by flying glass and many complained of shock and bruises. Two wagons were smashed and the line was strewn with debris. Services were delayed for quite some time. Passengers left the train and completed their journey by tramcar.

Although the CLC was without doubt a well managed and well run little concern, its passenger rolling stock was beginning to look a trifle ancient by the mid-1930s. The most modern coaching stock were 45 bogie vehicles built at Dukinfield in 1914 by J. G. Robinson. In 1937 it was decided that new

stock would have to be obtained for the Liverpool service. These appeared as four twin articulated units per set, with an overall length of about 427ft and a total weight of 192 tons. They were designed by Sir Nigel Gresley and built by the Craven Railway Carriage & Wagon Co Ltd of Sheffield.

In the circumstances perhaps the CLC may be forgiven for putting on something of a show. On Friday 9 April 1937 a trial run was organised between Manchester Central and Liverpool Central with stops at Warrington and Farnworth (not to be confused with Farnworth near Bolton). Before

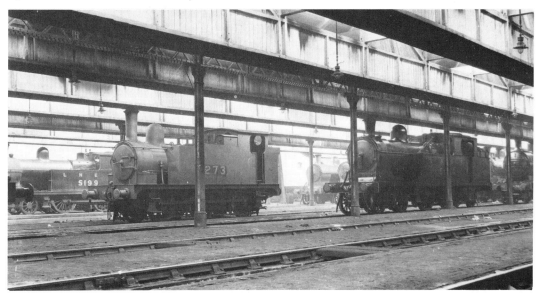

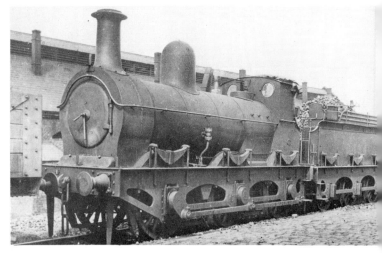

departure official guests were received by Mr G. Leedham, the Manager & Secretary of the CLC. The Lord Mayor was prevented from being present by a prior engagement in London, his place being taken by Sir Norton Barclay, Chairman of the Manchester & District Bank.

The train departed behind 'B17' No 2824 *Lumley Castle* with Driver E. A. Calvert of Gorton at the regulator. With an extra coach added the 220-ton train covered the 10.7 miles between Trafford Park and Padgate at an average speed of 73mph, a top speed of 80mph being touched just before slowing for Padgate Junction. At Warrington a stop of 40min was made to receive The Mayor and other dignitaries. The Mayor spoke appreciatively of the enterprise of the CLC and the excellence of the new rolling stock. Toasts were drunk and suitably acknowledged by Mr Leedham and Mr Harold Craven, the managing director of

the Craven Company. At Farnworth, six miles further on, The Mayor and Mayoress of Widnes led other notable citizens for a conducted tour of the train.

Although heavy traffic subsequently prevented any very fast running, Liverpool was reached at the appointed time of 2.00pm. There the Lord Mayor gave a reception and among the many prominent guests were Mr F. Liddell Steel, a director of the LNER and CLC, and Mr A. Harold Bibby DSO, also a director of the LNER. The new train entered regular service on the following Monday 12 April, being utilised on three return trips daily.

Below:
Superheated 'J11' No 5237 at Wigan in 1944.
Great Central Railway Society Collection.

5 Central

LNER

To follow the story of CLC motive power with that of the LNER seems a fairly logical step, although in fact the Midland were first on the scene by some 11 years, the GC line between Fairfield and Chorlton Junction not having been opened until October 1891; albeit only as far as Fallowfield in the first instance. Soon after grouping the services along this line settled into a pattern which would continue more or less unchanged until the outbreak of hostilities in 1939. There were seven up locals, two of which did not run on Saturday evenings, and an additional service at lunchtime on Saturdays. A similar service ran on the down line. It was the most sparse of local services from any of Manchester's main line stations and indeed it must be debatable whether or not the line had ever really justified a local service at all. Of course those were the days when trains were run purely as a 'social service' to the public. However, this meagre service was of

considerable interest to juvenile spotters of the day because, with Gorton shed having absolutely no inhibitions whatsoever with regard to tender engines running tender first on passenger trains, five up locals were worked by express passenger engines either making their way back in the direction of Gorton or on filling in turns. Three of the down locals were similarly powered, two with engines off shed working down to Manchester to pick up express trains and one filling in time. The first down local and return working, along with the lunchtime extra train on Saturdays were worked by an 'N5' which during the day worked a pick-up

Below:
Gorton 'B2' No 5427 *City of London* departs from Platform 2 at Central with a Liverpool express in July 1927. *W. Potter*

from Guide Bridge to Wilbraham Road, calling at Fallowfield and Levenshulme. Generally the locals terminated at Guide Bridge, however one was extended to Stalybridge and the second down in the morning and last up in the evening commenced and terminated at Fairfield from 1930 onwards. Normally the morning and lunchtime trains were worked by GC engines of Classes D10, D11, B2 and B3, although until well into the 1930s 'B7s' also appeared on these turns quite frequently. During the 1920s and early 1930s it was also a quite common occurrence to find an ex-works engine having a run; especially on the 8.40am arrival into Central. This engine then took charge of the 9.25am Hull service, a train noteworthy in that it called at Fallowfield to pick up. The 2.29pm arrival was brought in by the engine intended to work the up or eastbound Liverpool-Harwich Boat Train. The down Boat Train was remanned at Guide Bridge, and after arrival at Manchester the engine ran out to Trafford Park for servicing, returning to Manchester to work the 4.28pm up local, a return local and the 6.28pm up local. In later years a different passenger engine took the last local and the Boat Train engine then worked the 7.22pm up to Leicester.

Normally there were six up and seven down fast trains. During the summer season there was an increase of four trains on Saturday to and from the East Coast resorts. During the summer there was also an additional train to Cleethorpes on Monday, Friday and Saturday. A further additional arrival on a Friday, with a return working on Saturday during the season was the Orient Line Boat Train. This ran

for many years and was an Immingham working. The Harwich Boat Train was worked on alternate days by Gorton and Ipswich, the 7.45pm arrival, the 'crack' 3.20pm down from Marylebone, on alternate days by Neasden and Gorton. Morning arrivals at 9.57am and 10.20am were usually Neepsend turns, although there was a period in the early 1930s when the latter was worked through by a Leicester engine and crew. The remainder were Gorton workings until well into the middle 1930s when the arrivals at 11.16am and 12.10pm were Neepsend workings for a period. Of the two earlier arrivals in the morning, one engine went forward to Liverpool returning to Sheffield via the Tiviot Dale line, while the other departed Central with the 11.22am up Barnetby. A further Neepsend turn travelled to Liverpool via Tiviot Dale, on to Manchester with the eastbound Boat Train, and finally back to Sheffield with the 4.48pm up Hull. Yet another Neepsend turn worked around the triangle in the same direction, arriving at Manchester in good time to turn and work the 10.30pm up mail as far as Sheffield. The 4.48pm up Hull commenced the journey at Liverpool and comprised the set of stock which had arrived in Liverpool as the Boat Train. The set returned from Hull to Liverpool the following morning, arriving in time to form the eastbound Boat Train. The Boat Train, the 4.48pm up Hull and the 5.35pm up London on Sundays were smartly timed trains running non-stop between Manchester and Sheffield. For a period during the early 1930s the morning Hull-Liverpool via Tiviot Dale was diverted to run via the Fallowfield line. However the train did not run into Central, but instead took the left hand curve at Throstle Nest Junction and joined the Liverpool line at Trafford Park Junction alongside the Manchester United Football Ground. During this time the arrival times at Warrington and Liverpool were unchanged.

Below:
Caprotti valve 'B3' No 6168 *Lord Stuart of Wortley* at Gorton in April 1936, after removal of the cambox covers. *R. W. Hinton*

Above:
'D11' No 5501 *Mons* coaled up and ready to go in April 1936.
N. E. Preedy

Left:
Brunswick 'B7' No 5037 with original cylinders, passing Padgate Junction with a No 2 express goods, in the late 1930s.
Great Central Railway Society Collection

Below left:
Leicester Atlantic No 5264 awaiting shopping in May 1935.
W. Potter

Ipswich 'B17' No 2825 *Raby Castle* is ready for the Boat Train at Gorton in March 1939. Note the well stocked tender. *W. Potter*

For many years the Neepsend turns were handled with great verve and gusto by the 'C1' large-boilered GN Atlantics; the 4.48pm and 10.30pm up trains almost exclusively so. There was a short period during the early 1930s when one of the morning arrivals would be headed by a 'D9' 4-4-0, and in later years both morning trains were frequently 'Director'-hauled. Neepsend had one or two 'B17' 4-6-0s during 1937 and one of these turned up occasionally. During the period when Leicester engines were working the 10.20am arrival the GC Atlantics had the job virtually to themselves. Indeed the only occasion on which I noted anything other than an Atlantic was 8 September 1933 when 'D9' 4-4-0 No 6021 *Queen Mary* appeared. She was enjoying a very brief stay at Leicester at this time, but I have no information as to whether she was the rostered engine or a last minute replacement for a failed Atlantic.

The 11.16am and 12.10pm arrivals were brought in by engines which had gone up from London Road at 1.40am and 8.20am. During the 1920s and early 1930s these turns, which were in the Gorton No 2 link, were most frequently hauled by 'B2' 4-6-0s, with a fair number of 'Directors' and 'B7' 4-6-0s also appearing. Indeed I recall that during the winter of 1931/32 the 11.16am was 'B7'-hauled for two or three weeks running. The most frequent performers on these trains during the period from 1933 to 1935 were the 'B3' 4-6-0s of which the two Caprotti valved engines, *Earl Haig* and *Lord Stuart of Wortley* were the most often seen. As often as not they would be back in Central in the evening. One would leave Gorton at 6.20pm coupled to the engine for the 7.50pm No 1 braked goods from Deansgate to York, arriving at Central in time to go forward with the 7.22pm up Leicester. The other having gone forward to Sheffield with the 5.00pm London Road-Cleethorpes, would return to Central with the Hull-Liverpool which was due in Manchester at 9.50pm. After a visit to Gorton she would be ready to commence a new day with the 1.20am ex-London Road. Meanwhile her sister engine would be on her way back to London Road in time to run out to Gorton and back before starting all over again with the 8.20am up. From July-September there was a variation to the usual working; an extra train ran to Cleethorpes on Monday, Friday and Saturday during these months and on Monday and Friday this train was usually worked by the engine which had arrived with the 12.10pm. Gorton then provided an alternative engine for the 7.22pm.

No doubt many enthusiasts, particularly younger ones, looked upon the Harwich Boat Train as the highlight of the day. After through engine working between Ipswich and Manchester commenced in 1927, it did bring a little more variety to the scene: first with the ex-Great Eastern 'B12' 4-6-0s, and then with the 'B17s'; for a year or two this being the only 'B17' working. Nevertheless, although it ran quite smartly, especially between Liverpool, Manchester and Sheffield, it called at a few unlikely spots such as Worksop, Spalding, March and Bury St Edmunds, which in my view hardly lent it 'crack' train status. When through engine working first commenced, Gorton received 'B12' No 8557 with which to work the train, this locomotive being replaced after 12 months by No 8538. So far as I have been able to ascertain, Gorton drivers found these 'foreigners' reasonably satisfactory, whilst the firemen, in common with most strangers to the class, found it a rather long walk from the tender to the firebox!

A further 12 months or so went by and the first 'Sandringham' (B17) 4-6-0s arrived at Gorton. It is no secret that the 'Sandringhams' were not an immediate unqualified success and for the first year or two the 'B12s' reappeared from time to time. In particular I have a note of several appearing during 1930 when No 8531 was working the Gorton end. It is generally accepted that No 2802 *Walsingham* was first to be allocated to Gorton. I did not see her on this occasion, and after only a brief spell she was moved to Parkston Quay, her place being taken by No 2809 *Quidenham* which stayed for about 18 months before she in turn was replaced by No 2801 *Holkham*. These three were all equipped with the Westinghouse Brake. When No 2816 *Fallodon* (the first of the class without the Westinghouse equipment) appeared she was sent to Gorton; No 2801 moving back to the Great Eastern, after only about four months. Some eight months later *Fallodon*; was joined at Gorton by No 2834 *Hinchingbrooke*; not before time in my opinion as there must have been an element of risk in working the Boat Train without a reserve engine.

When after a further two years Nos 2840 *Somerlayton Hall*, 2841 *Gayton Hall* and 2842 *Kilverstone Hall* arrived at Gorton also, one began to wonder if the writing was on the wall for some of the old favourites. Five months later No 2824 *Lumley Castle* was a further addition to the ranks; she would appear to have been even less popular at Gorton than her sister engines. My records show that during her time at Gorton she did not appear to take her share of the top link turns. However all was not immediately lost for the older engines. At the close of 1934 Nos 2824 and 2842 were despatched to Neasden for 18 months and No 2834 for 12 months. Later, in 1935 No 2840 followed them but she was back at Gorton after a couple of months. Personally I have always held the opinion that the 'Sandringhams' were some of the most handsome looking engines ever produced, a view shared by most enthusiasts I have met. It was perhaps a pity that their maximum performance did not quite match their looks and it was unfortunate that they rode so badly.

Meanwhile, at the other end of the run Ipswich initially had Nos 2806 *Audley End* and 2807 *Blickling* (both fitted with Westinghouse brakes) working over to Manchester. In due time they received Nos 2820 *Clumber*, 2821 *Hatfield House* and 2825 *Raby Castle* and one of this trio then usually had the turn although the others continued to appear from time to time, as did No 2804 *Elveden* after she was transferred to Ipswich in 1932. It is thought No 2827 *Aske Hall* enjoyed a brief spell at Ipswich during the winter of 1933 during which time she made one trip on the train. She also made one trip during 1936 when she was at Parkston Quay. The final leg of the journey between Ipswich and Harwich was made by a Parkston Quay engine, usually a 'Sandringham' I understand. The reason for the change is not absolutely clear. Presuming the enginemen signed on between 12.30 and 1.00pm, they would be due for relief by the time Ipswich was reached at

8.41pm. One might ask why a second set of men could not take over as they did at Guide Bridge in the reverse direction, and this I believe brings us to the root of the problem: shortage of coal in the small GE pattern tenders. After leaving Gorton, the working of the 1.56pm Guide Bridge-Manchester local followed by the run to Ipswich would have resulted in a distance well in excess of 200 miles having been covered. Rather more I fancy than GE engines might expect to travel at a stretch and this, of course, included the slog over the Pennines. As a general rule Gorton worked the whole week with

Below:
March 'B4' 6104 photographed on 16 June 1935. This engine substituted most efficiently for the other motive power on the Boat Train on a couple of occasions. *L. Hanson*

the same locomotive. Indeed as already indicated they had little option for some time, a spare engine not being available. After the arrival of No 2834 the one engine a week remained the norm, exceptions to this being rare indeed. Ipswich on the other hand usually had the same engine coming to the west on Monday and Friday and a different engine on Wednesday. During 1935 Ipswich received No 2845 *The Suffolk Regiment* in exchange for No 2821, and from the outset No 2845 became something of a favourite. So much so that after the first week of 1936 she was to be seen on the train every week until entering the works for overhaul in October, and in 1937 she appeared every week.

The reliability of the class on the train was very good. Over a period of 3,300 sightings the failure rate was only about 1.8%. An ailing engine usually managing to complete her trip with replacement

being made at either Ipswich or Gorton. On odd occasions this proved impossible and something interesting would then turn up, such as March 'B4' No 6104 arriving on Saturday 3 March 1933 in place of No 2834; the same 'B4' also arrived with the train on Wednesday 6 February 1935. As this was an Ipswich day one can only guess which 'B17' had let the side down. The 'B4' returned with the eastbound train in normal course. Christmas Eve

Below:
Gorton's 'D10' No 5433 *Walter Burgh Gair*, on shed in April 1936. *R. W. Hinton*

Bottom:
Another Gorton favourite was 'D11' No 5503 *Somme*, the last 'Director' to move away in the autumn of 1939. In the rear is '04' No 6188, which spent 33 years at Mexborough. *N. E. Preedy*

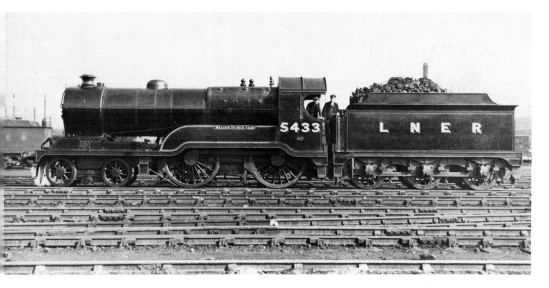

1934, a day on which the operating department could do without failures, saw the train arrive very late behind Neepsend 'B7' No 5033. During March 1937 things became a little complicated. On Thursday 6 March No 2861 took the up train in place of No 2845; No 2820 came back on the 7th; No 2845 returned home on the 8th; Monday the 10th saw No 2820 work the Gorton turn up and on 11 March No 2861 returned home.

During the high season of 1933/34 an extra train departed from Central at 9.33am on Saturdays for Ipswich and Harwich. The Ipswich locomotive which had come down with the Boat Train on the Friday returned with this extra train. The Boat Train was then worked forward by a Gorton passenger engine, it is believed only as far as Sheffield.

For a good many years Trafford Park had the responsibility of working the westbound on to Liverpool. After the diagram alterations of December 1936 a Gorton engine was employed. On 4 October 1937, 'K3' 2-6-0 No 3817 was entering Platform 1 at Liverpool Central with the Boat Train when her leading offside steps struck the platform coping stones. Some damage to the stones resulted as did damage to the steps and cylinder casing on the locomotive. A second Gorton 'K3' No 2417 took over the diagram: what she was doing in Liverpool at the time I have not discovered. The following day *Hinchingbrooke* was diagrammed for the trip to Liverpool, but it was found desirable to replace her with 'D11' No 5509 *Prince Albert* at

Guide Bridge at 12.45 when she would normally have been remanned. A few weeks later on 1 November, 'K3' No 3815 had proceeded to Liverpool with the Boat Train and her return trip was worked by 'D6' No 5871. On the following day No 2862 *Manchester United* was replaced on the Liverpool leg of the Harwich train by No 5871. It is not clear whether No 2862 had developed a last minute fault or if it was expected that No 3815 would be returned. In the event 'D9' No 6033 took over the diagram.

The other 'Star Turn' was the famous 3.20pm down from Marylebone. My signalman friend at Wilbraham Road considered this to be the 'crack' train, a view shared by many, especially old GC employees. In my experience always referred to in the Manchester Area as the 'Sam Fay' or perhaps more affectionately simply the 'Sam', I cannot be certain of the origin of this name. My erstwhile friend had it that at one stage Sir Sam Fay himself used the train regularly over the early portion of the journey. When I first saw the train in about 1927, it was 'Director' hauled as I would think it had been throughout the 1920s. By now it was usually a 'D11' working although Neasden continued to use a 'D10' occasionally until 1932. By this time Gorton only seemed to use a 'D10' in an emergency and usually only for one round trip. The exception being No 5433 *Walter Burgh Gair*, which must have been considered a bit special as she was still being rostered for a week now and then in 1934. May 1937 brought a diagram change which resulted in Gorton working the train daily. Prior to this date the Neasden engine returned home with the 2.20pm up from London Road on Tuesday, Thursday and Saturday. The Gorton engine which went south on Monday, Wednesday and Friday took the 3.50pm from London Road. The favourite at Neasden must have been Class D11 'Director' 4-4-0 No 5505 *Ypres*. Certainly she must have put in more

Below:
Trafford Park 'B9' No 6106 backing off shed in July 1939. Note the line of Bolsover coal wagons in the background. Private owner wagons were very much a part of the prewar scene, adding a blaze of colour when freshly painted. *W. Potter*

appearances than any of the others, if only because of her long uninterrupted stay at the shed as mentioned previously. She certainly headed the list of sightings in my records, No 5507 *Gerrard Powys Dewhurst* coming second. During the months when Nos 2824, 2840 and 2842 were at Neasden, I do not believe they were used on the 'Sam', although I cannot be certain, although on two separate occasions No 2842 arrived with the train on a Gorton day, deputising for the rostered engine. The first recording I have of a 'B17' on the 'Sam' was Wendesday 15 June 1933 when No 2841 had the job. Unfortunately I had not seen the train on the Monday and she may have appeared then. On the Saturday, however, 'D10', No 5438 *Worsley-Taylor* brought the train down. From then on until the diagram change in 1937 my sightings of the train revealed that 70% were 'B17'-worked. Neasden was allocated three 'B17s' in 1936 but remained almost constant with the 'Directors' until they lost the job in 1937. Less than 3% of my Neasden sightings were 'Sandringhams' ('B17's), most of

which if not all, were during July and August 1936 when they received their three of the 'Footballer' batch, Nos 2856/7/8. Almost immediately No 2847 exchanged places and tenders with No 2858.

It has been suggested that the 'B3' 'Valour' engines devoured so much coal that they would be unable to last out the run from Marylebone to Manchester. This of course is nonsense. They had worked the trips in earlier years, and in 1932 No 6164 and 6166 worked the 'Sam' down from Neasden on odd occasions. No 6164 did so again in 1933, 1934 and 1938. They were odd trips and probably the 'D11' rostered to the turn had been found wanting.

Before we leave the LNER passenger scene there are a further three locals to consider, two of which were rather unusual in so much as they were worked by Trafford Park engines. The 7.43am up returning from Guide Bridge at 8.43am was not only normally in charge of a Trafford 'C13' 4-4-2T, it was made up with seven CLC six-wheelers. The 5.43pm up returning at 6.55pm was a Trafford 'J10'

Left:
Mexborough 'K2' No 4632 in Gorton yard in September 1937.
W. Potter

Gorton 'K3' No 153 on shed in June 1938. Doncaster '04' No 6504 in the rear. *W. Potter*

turn as a general rule, my notes rather suggest that in the period 1927-31 it may have been in charge of a 'D7' 4-4-0 quite frequently. Subsequently a 'D2' or 'D6' might appear on the train, but only rarely. The third train which arrived in Central at 6.30pm was unusual because it was the only down local which the engine worked chimney leading. There was of course a good reason for this variation from the normal. After arrival at Manchester the engine, a 'J39' from about 1929 onwards, ran back to Trafford Park sidings where it arrived the right way round to work a class 'A' goods train to Lincoln at 7.50pm, joining the Chorlton line at Throstle Nest South Junction hard on the heels of the 7.50pm Deansgate-York No 1 Braked Goods.

The goods yards at Central and Deansgate generally had something to offer the observer. Towards the end of the 1920s the Great Eastern 'J69' 0-6-0Ts were introduced to the area; thereafter about a dozen might be found around the CLC sheds. At Trafford I have notes of Nos 7191/ 7198/7273/7351/7363/7371 and 7383 being in the vicinity in the 1930s. In the first instance they had replaced the Great Northern 'J52' shunting Deansgate but subsequently could also be seen at Central goods. No 7354, sometimes at Liverpool Walton, turned up at Gorton in the mid-1930s where it is thought to have been employed for a time as works shunter. NE 'J72' 0-6-0Ts Nos 2184/ 2307 and 2320 were tried at Wrexham and Bidston during the 1930s, but not, it is thought, with any success. No 2320 came on to Trafford Park but again does not seem to have been very much used. She was noted on Gorton shed on 6 April 1940.

Deansgate yard had useful pickings for the spotter, there were part-fitted trains, usually quite lengthy affairs to and from Colwick, some of which were in fact to or from King's Cross. These were worked on alternate days by Trafford Park and Colwick depots. Originally the motive power had been the GN 'J6' 0-6-0s, a stud being maintained at Trafford Park for this work. 1927/28 saw them replaced by GC 'B9' 4-6-0s, Colwick receiving an allocation of 'B8' inside-cylinder 4-6-0s also of GC origin. These two classes would appear to have been intended as mixed traffic engines, but by the 1930s they were seldom found on passenger turns, with the exception of occasional excursion work. The 'B9' in particular seemed incapable of running at anything approaching a decent speed. The Trafford ones were often employed on excursions to Southport at busy periods, a duty on which I can personally state they performed with a singular lack of distinction. Indeed I have had a better ride to Southport behind a 'J10' and an infinitely better one from Southport with a 'J11'. Nevertheless they performed admirably for quite a long period of time on the Colwick goods turns. No doubt a case of 'horses for courses'. In the early part of their time on

these trains it was rare indeed for Trafford to provide anything else, although later on a 'J39' would appear from time to time and very occasionally a 'K3'. Colwick on the other hand were always likely to send down the odd 'J6' but only infrequently a 'J39' or 'K3'. The smaller GN 'K2' Moguls would also appear from Colwick just occasionally. Trafford were quite likely to use one of the 'B8' engines on a little local work on the odd occasion, indeed a trip to Liverpool with a semi-fast was not unknown. Inevitably one would fail now and again and be replaced by a 'B8' or 'B9' according to which end of the trip a substitute was required. The original was not always immediately put back into her diagram. There was a turn from Colwick to Liverpool via Tiviot Dale; I recall a 'B8' arriving at Liverpool and being used on one occasion on the Manchester services for best part of a week at least. I can say with confidence that Colwick must have adopted the same practice. As many readers will no doubt be aware, Colwick supplied the motive power for excursion trains run from the old GN terminus at Belgrave Road, Leicester to the East Coast resorts. I once took an excursion from Belgrave Road to Mablethorpe and had a rather miserable ride there and back behind a 'B9'.

There was a further Colwick turn in each direction which took a rather strange route. The up train departed at 8.25pm, took the Midland line at Chorlton Junction and as a general rule travelled via Dore and Chinley to Chesterfield, thence via Codnor Park. It is believed that on occasions this train travelled via Ambergate and the Butterley line. Nothing larger than a 0-6-0 was allowed on account of the trestle bridge near Codnor Park.

There can be no doubt that the 'Star Turn' among the goods trains from the observer's point of view was the 5.50pm ex-Deansgate No 1 Braked Goods to York. Although I cannot be definite my notes suggest that this train commenced running on 7 May 1934. Memory, not always as reliable as it might be, tends to agree that the train was not running in earlier years. This view is further supported by the sightings of a similar train departing from Deansgate at 7.50pm. Neither of these trains ran on a Saturday, when there was a Class 'B' goods to York at 5.20pm. The 5.50pm was a most interesting working. From Tuesday to Friday it appeared to be a Doncaster job, but quite often engines from other GN sheds would appear and engines of class 'B15', 'B16' and 'K3' from the North Eastern area as well. On a Monday Gorton usually provided the engine which was usually a 'J39'. At the outset Doncaster sent down 'K1' or 'K2' Moguls with only a few 'K3s'. As the years rolled by the incidence of the 'K3' grew ever higher and the numbers of the smaller engines gradually decreased. Doncaster also sent down a few 'J39s' and once or twice a year one of their three 'B17s', Nos 2832 *Belvoir Castle*, 2833 *Kimbolton Castle* and 2835 *Milton*. The 7.50pm was without doubt nominally a Gorton working, nevertheless of the 100 sightings immediately prior to the 5.50pm which appear in my notes, 26 were 'foreign' engines, largely Moguls, but also a 'B17' and two 'B16s'.

The working timetable also listed a class 'A' goods to York at 11.00pm. Memory suggests that this train ran only infrequently, perhaps only as required, this is supported by my notes. When the train was sighted a 'foreign' engine appeared on 72% of such sightings. Other regular visitors to Deansgate came from Ardsley and Lincoln. Mineral trains were usually bound for Trafford Park sidings and in the main were hauled by 'O4' 2-8-0s, or the occasional 'Q4' 0-8-0s.

A large percentage of the LNER excursion traffic was routed to Central, for not only was there usually more space available, but often there would be a Liverpool connection. For many years such trains to the East Coast resorts, race meetings and football matches were the almost exclusive province of the 'B7' 4-6-0s. Very occasionally a 'B2' 4-6-0 might appear. Needless to say, later years brought a change, the 'K3' 2-6-0s being the usual motive power, although 'B17s' were not unknown. During the season for many years a train titled 'The Orient Line Special' arrived in Central at about lunchtime on Friday, returning early on Saturday afternoon. This was an Immingham working, but did not offer much motive power variety. My earlier notes show a 'D9' in charge. The load is not indicated therefore I cannot guess whether or not a pilot would have been required over Woodhead. If one had been provided it would probably have come off at Guide Bridge. Subsequently the 'B7s' were again very prominent, with the occasional 'B2s' or 'B3s'. Indeed, 'B3' No 6164 *Earl Beatty* worked the train for four weeks running during 1936. On one occasion in 1935 'K2' No 4644 turned up — she was a March engine at the time. 'B4' No 6104 appeared once in 1937 and 'B4' No 6095 once in 1938. Both were Lincoln engines. One expects the occasional failure along the way, as undoubtedly was the case on one occasion in 1938 when Neepsend's 'D10' No 5438 *Worsley-Taylor* arrived 120min late. Also during 1938 Immingham unusually sent 'C4' No 5358 which had only recently arrived at the shed. So far as I am aware the experiment was not repeated.

When it was found necessary to provide a pilot for the run over Woodhead, in the case of trains bound for Central, the pilot would be dropped at Guide Bridge unless it was required in Central for a return working. Sometimes, the Hull-Liverpool due at Central at 9.50pm was often an example, the train engine would take the lead at Sheffield, come

off on arrival at Guide Bridge and run light to Gorton. The pilot would then carry on to Central, turn, and pilot to Sheffield on the 10.30pm.

Railway Queen Day at Belle Vue invariably brought a goodly supply of 'foreign' engines, sometimes including a 'B12', as indeed happened on the day the Rechabites occupied Belle Vue. On that day too, both the original 'B1' engines came down the Fallowfield line, quite possibly the only occasion on which that happened in LNER days.

I have not traced any serious accident on the LNER line into Central. There was an occasion when I was spending a Monday afternoon watching the usual 'N5' No 5532 shunting the yard at Wilbraham Road. Suddenly, very quietly, with no sign of fuss or bother, she gently derailed, just fouling the up main line. Mid-afternoon was a quiet period, sometimes there would be an occasional goods, but not on this day as it happened. The up Boat Train had to run wrong road from Chorlton Junction to Wilbraham Road behind No 2824 *Lumley Castle* (one of her rare appearances on the train) and the Gorton crane had No 5532 back on the rails before the up local passed at 4.40pm.

Infinitely more exciting was the occasion when the down Boat Train almost came to grief at Chorlton Junction. An inexperienced signalman at the junction accepted a down LMS local due to pass at 1.52pm and then immediately accepted the Boat Train; the latter was most unusually running about 7min late. The Boat Train passed Wilbraham Road travelling far faster than it ought to have been, it was evident that the statutory 20mph restriction around the junction curve was intended to be interpreted rather liberally. The junction distant situated on a short post to the left of the track would not come into the driver's view until the last seconds owing to track curvature through the station at Wilbraham Road. In normal circumstances this would be no great handicap as the brakes would already be hard on for the approaching speed restriction. In this instance no doubt the driver was astonished to find the distant against him, for he was going to have little chance of pulling up in time from the speed at which he was travelling. Meanwhile the LMS local in charge of a 'Flat Iron' 0-6-4T was perhaps some 300yd from the junction when the driver, alerted by the screaming whistle of the Boat Train engine, spotted the express coming into view to the right of his train. Fortunately, travelling at the usual speed of the LMS locals he would have no difficulty in stopping before arriving at the junction. There was a little panic going on in the junction box, with signals being hastily changed and points moved, hopefully before the express actually arrived on the spot. In fact *Raby Castle* and her tender were certainly over the points before she came to rest, as was part of the first coach if my memory serves me correctly.

6 Central

LMS

From early childhood I had an affection for Central station which remains even today. This stems no doubt from what are among my earliest and happiest memories. When I was very young my family had moved from Leicester (my birthplace) to Manchester. Thereafter and for many years trips to and from Leicester were made at frequent intervals. In my boyhood such trips were usually made by the Midland Route. At a very early age I grew to love the line, especially the stretch between Chinley and Ambergate. To me this was the most beautiful line in all England and certainly the most exciting to ride over. Although the frequent curves in the line prohibited the highest speeds, nevertheless those same curves with the frequent cuttings and tunnels gave an illusion of high speed and all added up to a most exciting experience for a young boy and one of which I never tired. My earliest recollections go back to about 1923/24, when the express trains

were always hauled by what my father informed me were 'Compound' engines, although he liked to refer to them by their then familiar name of 'Crimson Ramblers'. At busy times these engines would be assisted by an engine of similar appearance except it would have inside cylinders. These assisting engines were of course the '2P' 4-4-0 engines which were later multiplied by the LMS. Whether or not I ever rode on a train when the pilot was an older or smaller engine than a '2P' I cannot now say, but I do recall seeing such engines at Derby and Leicester. In 1927, when we moved to a spot quite near the Midland line, nothing smaller

Below:
Nottingham (16A) 'Compound' No 927 at Central in May 1937. *W. Potter*

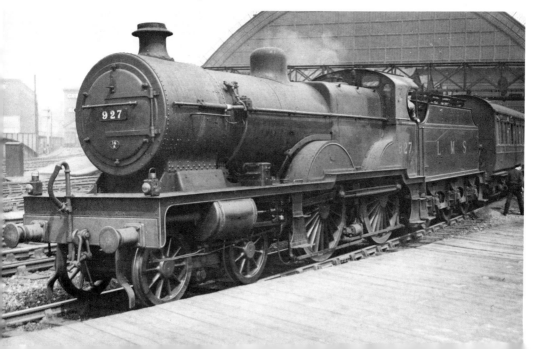

than a '2P' was likely to be found on the Manchester side of Derby; it is from this time that my story of Manchester and the Midland really begins.

The 'Compounds' were still in charge of the express trains and indeed would continue unchallenged for a further eight years, still of course being assisted as soon as the load exceeded the magical tonnage figure laid down at Derby. To digress, I have in later years had very good runs behind 'Compounds' pulling loads in excess of what Derby would have considered suitable, not always with the younger LMS built engines, and on at least two occasions over the stiff Peak Forest line. During the 1930s at holiday times, trains on this route (as on most others) ran in two and, even on the odd occasion, three portions. Generally all the portions would be double-headed. I have to confess I never succeeded in solving these double-heading arrangements: a pair of engines arriving seldom seemed to return together. For many years if Trafford Park had to find a pilot for a departure it had to be another 'Compound', no other type of passenger engine being maintained at the depot. For a long time the stud at Trafford consisted of ex Midland 7ft engines Nos 1014-1022 and LMS-built 6ft 9in engines Nos 1089 and 1090. I cannot be absolutely certain but I believe Nos 1014 and 1015 moved away with the arrival of the two newer engines. All of these would take their turn on the London trains which all seemed to change engines at Derby. This did not mean that Trafford men did not get to London. At least one diagram worked a

slow train to Derby and then took over an express to St Pancras. The first time I recall using the train as a boy I was rather disappointed when a Trafford engine backed on at Derby. A consequence of this system was that Kentish Town engines were rather rare in Manchester until the advent of the Stanier engines when through working became the norm.

Derby 'Compounds' were of course regular visitors and occasionally a Sheffield example might appear. There were three regular Nottingham 'Compound' turns during the 1930s which at this time were worked by three of Nos 925-928 or 1093-1096. On 5 and 6 November 1936 the three arrived in sequence viz: 1094/95/96. It was I suppose almost inevitable that three consecutive numbered engines turned up from time-to-time; not often though in strict numerical sequence in order of arrival. Another interesting diagram during this period brought a Bristol 'Compound' down with a train from London which arrived at 9.52am. The locomotive departed with the up working at 12.20pm, coming off at Derby. My notes suggest that this was a Derby working in the 1920s. The Bristol engines at this time were, I believe Nos 1023-1031 and 1097/98. Derby naturally had quite a large allocation including I think Nos 1045-1050, 1057-1061 and 933-936. Latterly No 936 was running with a rather hideous looking tender probably a standard tender originally, it had been altered to resemble the Stanier type.

I would not like to state definitely which was the first Stanier tender engine to appear at Central — my first recording is of 'Black Five' No 5055 on 1 February 1935; a Kentish Town engine at the time if my memory serves me well. I should not be surprised if it were not the first ever. The first of the class I recorded bearing a Trafford Park shed plate was No 5067 on the day after, followed in the next few days by Nos 5068/69, 5035/36 and 5042. I has always been my belief that the authorities were

...ather hasty in banishing the 'Compounds' from the Midland section express trains. Nottingham's Nos 925-928 were barely eight years old when the Stanier engines first appeared and Derby's Nos 935 and 936 were not built until 1932. In my experience they were quite capable of handling the normal traffic, and although the 'Black Five' managed perfectly well from the start, Trafford Park men with whom I conversed complained that they used more coal and water. On the other hand when the '5XP' engines (the 'Jubilees') first came on the scene their average performance left a great deal to be desired if my journeys were anything to go by. I recall an occasion arriving in Central behind one when the driver, after a particularly dismal run, remarked that a good "Compound" could lose this thing'. The strange thing to my mind was what happened when holiday times came around. The Midland seemed obsessed with the idea that assistance must be provided. A rough guide in those days appeared to be 'if over eight provide a pilot'. The following table offers a comparison of August Bank Holiday sightings from 1935-38:

1935

744/5056	504/925	927/5068	744/925
419/928	744/5043	629/926	1058/925
418/555	744/933	735/1049	

1936

1020/5032	1029/1057	600/5038	559/5188
378/925	765/5180	514/1043	
1043/5035	1021/936	1072/5095	
600/931	1020/1001	1090/5067	

1937

756/5283	526/1058	1075/5265	1032/5036
516/1097	418/1095	548/1024	
516/5264	548/1021	1075/564	
526/935	1046/5283	424/5286	

1938

5262/5283	525/5612	726/5612	726/1038
504/5616	504/5709	378/5067	
1021/5664	525/5602	378/5618	
504/5036	1060/5641	504/5271	

The load rarely if ever exceeded 10 cars, yet in 1938 even the 'Jubilees' had the usual assistance. As late as 1947 I had an excellent run from Derby to Manchester behind No 1000 hauling 10 coaches, the elderly white-haired gentleman at the regulator was truly an artist among enginemen. Once indeed I travelled the same route on an excursion and No 1017 had 12 bogies, drew up at every stop, and experienced some difficulty starting south of Peak Forest. Inevitably some time was lost and she should have had assistance.

Sunday down expresses during the 1930s were very often loaded to 10 coaches. The engine would be a 'Crab' and I cannot recall assistance over being given. Strangely these large, ungainly looking machines found much favour among the Midland men: I never heard them faulted. Firemen especially seemed to enjoy their work on a 'Crab', claiming they were easy on coal and water on the Peak run.

There was a frequent service to and from Sheffield via the Dore and Chinley line. Most trains called at all stations and in a number of cases passengers were required to change at Chinley. Generally speaking these trains were worked by Class 2P 4-4-0s from Sheffield Millhouses. Once the Stanier engines were established on the Midland, 'Compounds' appeared more frequently on the Sheffield trains.

There was also a service of sorts to Buxton. Apart from on one or two trains for businessmen in the morning and evening on weekdays, or at lunchtime on Saturdays, passengers would again have to change trains en route, usually at Miller's Dale, where an 0-4-4T operated a motor train to and from Buxton, or occasionally perhaps at Chinley. The through trains were usually worked by Class 2P 4-4-0s from Buxton depot, but every now and again the scene in Central would be enlivened by the appearance from Buxton of a Longsight engine. I have records of Nos 5326 *W. C. Brocklehurst* and 5349 *British Empire* paying odd visits in early 1933. Early the following year No 5187 *Helvellyn* and No 1111 (a Longsight 'Compound') turned up, and during the summer of that year, Nos 5347 *Elkhound* and 5349 *British Empire* appeared. In October No 5383 *John Mayall* was observed, as was No 5187 *Helvellyn* in December. Finally, in the first quarter of 1936, Nos 5348 *Coronation*, No 5350 *India*, 5293 *Levens* and 5294 *Druid* were all frequent visitors over a couple of months or so — on numerous occasions two of them turning up on the same day. So far as I am aware the last two named were actually Crewe North engines. I have no record of 'foreign' engines on these jobs subsequently, but in 1937/38 Buxton 'Crabs' Nos 2773, 2930, 2937, 2939, 2940 and 2943 frequently replaced the usual '2P', and occasionally 'Prince' tanks would appear. These latter would be among the ones normally employed on the Buxton-London Road service. I have notes of Nos 2369, 2381 and 2382.

At Grouping the local services to Cheadle Heath and Stockport Tiviot Dale had been in the charge of ex-Midland 0-6-4Ts for some 16 years. Generally known as 'Flatirons', but often referred to in the Manchester area as 'Block Tanks', these worthies continued to work these trains in a capable if unspectacular fashion for a further 11 years or so. In my early days along the line, ex-L&Y 2-4-2Ts were tried on the locals; not it would seem with much success, as they did not reign for very long. I believe Nos 10901-10906 were involved and that a little earlier one or two others had also appeared for brief spells. So far as I recall one would be unlikely to see more than one or two at any one time. The 'Flatirons' at this time would be from Nos 2006-2010, and 2022. A little later on, probably after the departure of the last 2-4-2T, Nos 2004 and 2020 turned up. No 2019 arrived on the scene as late as November 1934, and my notes suggest she replaced No 2006. The *Railway Magazine* of March 1929 mentions No 2003 on the Manchester local services; she had without doubt figured in earlier days but I believe she had departed before 1929. During the winter of 1929/30 'Prince' tanks Nos 2372 and 2374 figured prominently and remained for some little time; these were new engines at this time and No 2373 is also supposed to have come new to Trafford Park. However, I have no record of the latter which leads me to suppose her stay to have been short lived.

19 October 1934 held a surprise, it was the first time that I saw a Stanier engine working out of Central, namely three-cylinder 2-6-4T No 2525. She was joined during the next few days by Nos 2526/27, and during December Nos 2532-36 also arrived, although in fact I have no record of the last one until 2 January 1935. These new engines made light work of the locals for a few weeks, the last five were observed working for the last time on 13 March 1935, Nos 2525/26 on 23 March and No 2527 the following day. Back to work came Nos 2004/07/08/09/10 and 2019 assisted in their labours after 23 March by 'Prince' tanks Nos 2372/ 73. This 'Indian Summer' of the 'Old Faithfuls' was to be short lived. A month later the first of the Stanier Class 3P 2-6-2Ts arrived, Nos 88 and 89 followed by Nos 77 and 78 and then Nos 93-96. When some months later Nos 141 and 142 turned up Nos 77 and 78 were sent to Macclesfield.

Meanwhile the 'Flatirons' were in the main moved on as the new engines arrived, Nos 2010 and 2019 being the last two in service on 30 May although No 2004 was observed lying dead on Trafford Park Shed as late as 1 February 1936. The new engines were of rather puny appearance and in my opinion rather puny performers also. They were certainly no improvement on the 'Flatirons' on these duties and certainly not as reliable. It was rare indeed to note a '4F' 0-6-0 on local passenger work prior to the arrival of the 2-6-2Ts; thereafter it was commonplace. For over 30 years these locals had been made up of specially designed sets of nine close-coupled bogies which fitted nicely alongside the intermediate station platforms. In the mid-1930s they were replaced by new sets of seven cars. Perhaps I am showing undue bias if I say memory seems to suggest this coincided with the introduction of the 2-6-2Ts. Before the end of the decade there was some further reshuffling of the stud. No 114 joined the ranks in March 1936 but along with No 96 departed at the end of April. No 97 had turned up on 18 April but also vanished at the end of the month. Towards the end of 1939 Nos 120 and 139 were noted in traffic for about four months and then No 113 turned up, at which juncture the powers that be decided that they could no longer continue the war effort without my assistance! A friend who visited Manchester in 1941 rode out to Didsbury behind No 112. The only notes I have of postwar workings rather suggest that the only Stanier 2-6-2Ts in use in 1946/47 were Nos 88, 89, 90 and 94.

If one travelled over the Peak line some goods traffic would be observed, though not perhaps on the scale of the Woodhead line. Little of this traffic came as far down as Chorlton. The only regular daily goods turns I recall were light mixed trains in either direction during the evening. For many years these were worked by '3F' 0-6-0s Nos 3612 and

3638. On the infrequent occasions either was missing a similar engine would appear, borrowed from Rowsley. The Midland goods depot in Manchester was at Ancoats, and was reached via the Great Central & Midland Joint line between Marple and Ashburys.

One interesting seasonal working into Central was a short train of bogie vans containing strawberrys from East Anglia, on which I rather think express lamps were carried. The train usually ran during the first fortnight in July and was invariably worked by a '2P' 4-4-0 from either Peterborough or Lincoln, thereby affording something in the way of a change.

During 1937 it was decided that the London services should be speeded up; with that in mind there took place an event on 22 April which was the occasion for a few brief moments of excitement. A special train of eight coaches (255 tons) was run in each direction, presumably to determine what might be achieved by the Stanier engines. A journey time of 3½ hours seems to have been the

Top:
'Flatiron', 0-6-4T No 2009 at Trafford Park in early 1935.
W. Potter

Above left:
'Flatiron' No 2004 at Heaton Mersey in April 1935. *W. Potter*

Left:
Stanier 2-6-2T No 94 at Heaton Mersey in April 1936. *W. Potter*

Above:

Deeley rebuild of an 1882 '2P', No 338, at Cheadle Heath in the early 1930s. *W. Potter*

target and the down run almost managed this despite having to pull up rather suddenly when leaving Derby: a member of the official party having alighted and failed to climb back aboard before the train started moving again. In charge of the train was 'Black Five' No 5278 in the hands of Driver W. Smith and Fireman H. Crooks of Trafford Park. Sometime ago I was given a snapshot of what is believed to be 5278 approaching the junction at Chorlton at high speed. Alas it is not a very clear picture, indeed the most striking thing about it is what appears to be part of the ashpan, firebars and fire of a preceding train lying between the metals!

On the return run Driver G. H. Beebe and Fireman R. Foulkes also of Trafford Park had No 5264 and had no difficulty in running to time. As a result some little improvement appeared in the timetables some months later. Four up trains were rescheduled to cover the trip in 3hr 20min, 3hr 38min, 3hr 45min and 3hr 47min. Three down trains were allowed 3hr 35min, 3hr 38min and 3hr 40min. On the face of it this was nothing very remarkable. Before 1914 there were trains booked to cover the journey in 3hr 35min including a 4min stop at Leicester and travelling via the avoiding line at Derby, reputedly worked by the '3P' Belpaire engines. The surprising thing surely is that it took so many years to achieve something similar.

A rather unusual mishap befell a goods train approaching Chorlton Junction along the up line

on 17 April 1932. A large transformer riding upon a bogie low-loader wagon suddenly fell through the wagon flooring on to the track. Throughout the night trains were delayed for about 20 min. The following morning, particularly during the rush-hour, saw considerable inconvenience and delay to most trains including those bound for London. The following March there was even more disruption when a wagon laden with limestone collapsed inside Peak Forest tunnel derailing three other wagons and scattering debris across both tracks. A second goods train entered the tunnel from the opposite direction and ran into the debris. There were no injuries but breakdown gangs from Derby and Manchester were at work throughout the day clearing up and checking the track. Trains between Derby and Manchester were diverted via Chesterfield and the Dore and Chinley line.

On 25 February 1936 the 8.30am stopping train to Cheadle Heath ran into a stationary goods train as it was approaching Cheadle Heath station. The passenger train remained on the rails but several wagons left the track and blocked both up and down lines. Driver James Wood of Heaton Mersey received severe head injuries. Fireman Joseph Hampson had cuts and abrasions to the head. Passenger Mr F. Churwell of Monton, also received an injury to his head. On an outward bound local at this time of day one wonders if Mr Churwell was the only passenger. The lines were blocked for several hours and trains were diverted via Tiviot Dale. It has not been possible to identify the engine, although 2-6-2T No 89 does not appear to have been in use on the two days following the incident.

On 20 September 1936 considerable disruption and delay to train movements ensued when '2P' 4-4-0 No 400, a regular visitor from Millhouses Sheffield, left the rails just outside Central station. In due course '4F' 0-6-0 No 4476 arrived with a crane to sort out the mess.

Central

The Station

In a manner of speaking London Road could have been considered to be two stations under one roof. Central was quite different, trains belonging to the three companies making use of the facilities were not confined to their own sections, or even their own platforms. It is true to say that certain arrivals and departures were usually to be found alongside a particular platform, for instance Chester trains were often to be found at Platform 4, those for the St Helens and Southport lines at Platforms 1 or 2, and those for Liverpool at Platform 2, but this was by no means a hard and fast rule, especially in the case of the Liverpool trains. When I was a boy the St Pancras trains were usually to be found at Platform 3, but in later years were more likely to be found alongside Platform 6.

Observant travellers into and out of Central during the weeks preceding Sunday 23 June 1935 would have noticed certain work in progress along the approaches to the terminus. Enthusiasts would most likely have had foreknowledge of what was taking place, or would have drawn certain conclusions from their observations. 23 June dawned and with it came new signalling. The familiar semaphores had vanished, and had been replaced by colour lights. All the existing signalling between Manchester Central and Viaduct signalbox would be abolished, together with signalboxes designated Manchester Central 'A', 'B', Great Northern Junction and Viaduct. The new signalling would be controlled from a new cabin known as Manchester Central erected over the lines leading to Platforms 5, 6 and 7. The plan and instructions also revealed that the up 'A' and 'B' lines' starting signals, together with the down 'A' and 'B' lines' outer home signals and all those situated at Cornbrook West Junction, would also be replaced by colour light signals; these were to be controlled by Cornbrook West Junction Box. At this juncture it is worth remembering that the 'B' roads were the Liverpool tracks and also that when the Chorlton-

cum-Hardy line joined the CLC, the down line became the up line and vice versa. The new down signals at Cornbrook had telephones enabling enginemen to communicate with the West Junction Cabin and the up signals had a similar facility connected to the cabin at Central. The four main running lines between Manchester Central and Cornbrook West were equipped with track circuiting although the middle road, at the centre of the four running roads, is shown on the plan with no indication of track circuiting. The whole of Manchester Central yard and passenger station was track circuited throughout except for the centre roads between the platforms. All points were electrically operated from the new cabin and controlled by track circuits, with the exception of the crossovers between platform lines which were operated by ground frames protected by release control from the new cabin. Each signal carried a distinguishing number and either the letter 'M' or 'C', indicating the signal was controlled by Manchester or Cornbrook as appropriate. Also provided was a comprehensive system of route indicators for the information of drivers and others concerned. The centre road between Platforms 8 and 9, designated 'D' road, previously had direct connection with the turntable road, but this was removed.

Nothing untoward happened on the Sunday 23 June. One or two of Monday's papers made a brief mention of the changeover and one carried a report which included reference to a slight hitch in the proceedings during Sunday afternoon. During a period of about 20min trains had been signalled by flag between what was described as 'Liverpool Junction' (presumably Cornbrook West) and the terminus. A train from Sheffield had suffered a few minutes delay. Obviously only a relatively small number of trains would have been running on a Sunday afternoon.

Chester 'C13' No 5002, with Nottingham 'Compound' No 928 in the background, at Central in July 1937.
W. Potter

Monday 24 June was a very different story. No doubt there were many frayed tempers as the businessmen's trains began to run late during the morning rush hour. All seems to have gone reasonably smoothly until about 8.30am, after which it is thought both signalling and footplate staff found themselves insufficiently accustomed to cope with the new system. The position rapidly worsened and it is believed that something like forty trains were delayed during the next 3hr or so.

The longest delayed arrival was rather more than 30min down and the latest departure was the 9.28am for Chester which got away at 10.00am. One newspaper account attributed the delays to nervous tension among drivers unaccustomed to the new system. One reporter who claimed to have been inside the signalbox during the afternoon, described what he witnessed as 'Panic Stations'. There was one man supposedly standing in the centre of the box trying to decide what should move and to where, who was shouting instructions to two other men working the controls. Other newspaper items included such headlines as '400 trains in hold-up caused by signals', 'Expresses 2 hours late' and 'Locals 4 miles in an hour'. Rather unusually there do not appear to have been any photographs.

Before noon things were approaching normal. The worst might well have been over, but fate stepped in and administered another blow. Nottingham 'Compound' No 926, having duly arrived at 11.37am or very shortly after, eventually made her way towards the turntable and whilst so doing became derailed. Subsequent happenings can hardly be laid at the door of the new system, although the system undoubtedly contributed to the absolute chaos that followed. The immediate result was the blocking of the access to Platforms 6 to 9 and the turntable road. One or two engines and some stock were sealed in the platforms and five engines were trapped in the turntable area. One of these engines — 'B2' 4-6-0 No 5424 City of Lincoln had arrived off the GC line at 12.17pm and should have taken the 1.08pm stopping train to Guide Bridge. This train eventually got away at 2.10pm behind Trafford Park 'D2' 4-4-0 No 4381.

The results of the unfortunate mishap were immediate and dramatic. The 12.20pm St Pancras did not get away until about 1.45pm behind 'Black Five' No 5066. This engine had been something of a surprise when she came in with the 9.52am from St Pancras; for some years this train had been part of a Bristol diagram between Derby and Manchester and was normally worked by one of that shed's 'Compounds'. The Nottingham turns also continued to be worked by 'Compounds' for some time after Stanier's engines appeared. The 1.45pm St Pancras departed in rather better time than the 12.20, leaving at 2.30pm. For some time trains were arriving at the station approximately one hour

late. The train from St Pancras due at 12.50pm with 'Black Five' No 5042 was just on one hour behind. The next arrival from St Pancras due at around 2.30pm was standing at Chorlton-cum-Hardy, about 3½ miles out, for a very long time. Indeed it was reported that several passengers alighted and completed their journeys by tramcar. In the queue ahead of the London train were three locals and the westbound Continental Boat Train. This latter finally made Central just about an hour after the scheduled time of 1.53pm. 'B17' No 2801 Holkham, a Parkeston Quay engine was in charge, no doubt on loan to Ipswich at the time, three of the Ipswich 'B17' engines Nos 2807/20/21 being in Gorton works at this time. In fact when No 2821 left the works she was sent to March shed, No 2845, a new engine, having been sent to Ipswich. I have no record of the 12.30 or 1.30 departures for Liverpool and the Boat Train should have gone forward at 2.00pm. However a special was arranged and departed at 2.15pm, it is thought behind Northwich 'J10' No 5799. 'Compound' No 1096 eventually arrived in the station well over an hour late with the 2.30pm, followed by the eastbound Boat Train from Liverpool behind 'C1' No 3276. At this time I do not believe No 2816 Fallodon had arrived with the 2.29pm from Guide Bridge, I know she did not get the Boat Train away until 4.10pm, some 60min late.

Matters did not improve for several hours and later in the afternoon, it was announced that a 'Fog Service' would have to be brought into operation to deal with the evening rush-hour services. This on a brilliantly sunny afternoon with temperatures soaring into the 80s! No doubt the temperatures and tempers of intending passengers were also soaring. The 4.45pm Buxton did not depart until 6.13pm and it was reported that one incoming local took 70min to travel eight miles. Another train which left Trafford Park (2½ miles distant) at 5.00pm arrived in Central at 6.15pm to the tumultuous cheers of the passengers. The 2.20pm ex-St Pancras due 6.23pm was diverted via the Great Central & Midland Joint Line to London Road. In all, it was stated only 10 trains were cancelled, but that after 8.30am practically every train had been delayed to a greater or lesser extent.

During this time there was some goods traffic into the Central and Deansgate yards. For example, the 7.50pm York No 1 fitted departed behind 'B7' 4-6-0 No 5034 without incurring a great deal of delay. The 5.50pm York fitted did not run at all that week presumably due to insufficient traffic. The part-fitted trains to and from Colwick do not appear to have run either and may possibly have been diverted to Ashburys or Store Street.

Congestion continued to delay CLC and LMS trains until late on that Monday evening. However, fate had still one more blow to aim at Central before

Brunswick 'D9' No 5104 *Queen Alexandra* turning at Central in April 1936. *W. Potter*

this disastrous day was over. Shortly after 9.00pm a light engine coming off 'C' road (the centre road between Platforms 5 and 6) derailed on the points. Further complications ensued but did not cause disorganisation to the whole of the station. Nevertheless a number of workers were engaged in rerailing operations until a late hour.

During the late evening there was an unusual occurrence which could hardly be attributed to any of the unfortunate happenings of the day. An LNER train from Hull was due to arrive at 9.50pm. This was a Gorton turn, the engine being scheduled to go forward to Sheffield on the 5.00pm London Road departure for Cleethorpes. Coming off at Sheffield the engine had 145min to while away before departing for Manchester Central. Indeed I have a couple of records where she was back in Central at 7.45pm with the 'Sam Fay', the rostered engine having had to be relieved at Sheffield. To return to 24 June 1935, No 6168 *Lord Stuart of Wortley* was expected on the Hull arrival; she had brought the 11.16am in from Leicester and as far as I can judge had got away on time with the 12.10pm stopping train to Guide Bridge. However the 9.50pm arrived behind 'C4' Atlantic No 5363. This was a Leicester engine and would have picked up the diagram at Sheffield. The following day No 5427 *City of London* took over and No 6168 was not observed in Central again until the 27th.

After all the excitement and upset of such a day perhaps we might consider a normal day in the station, for example 24 September 1935. The observer is fortunate in that his place of employment is at a window overlooking the approach roads to the station, goods yard and the adjacent Deansgate yard. Travelling in from Didsbury behind Stanier Class 3P 2-6-2T No 88, we notice 'Black Five' No 5042 working an up local. Unlike Heaton Mersey, Trafford Park has no '4Fs'; if a tank engine is out of service a 'Compound' is the usual substitute (at this time, apart from the tank engines, Trafford Park only had 'Compounds' and 'Black Fives'). Before we arrive in Manchester we pass a local to Guide Bridge, surprisingly the usual 'N5' is missing, 'F2' 2-4-2T No 5782 taking her place. In the vicinity of Deansgate yard we observe 'B8' 4-6-0 No 5004 *Glenalmond*. She would have come down in the early morning with a No 2 part-fitted goods from Colwick. One would expect to see one or two 'J69' around the yards, and sure enough we note Nos 7371 and 7191; later in the morning we shall see No 7363 emerging from the depths of Deansgate yard. Having alighted from the train, we wait for a minute or two to watch the arrival of the local from Fairfield at 8.40am. 'D11' No 5511 *Marne* is in charge running tender first. Shortly she will depart with the Hull train at 9.25am. This train originates from Liverpool and on this occasion is brought over to Manchester by 'D9' No 5104 *Queen Alexandra*. Among the usual collection of tank engines of various varieties and of course Pollitt 'D6' engines, we note Trafford 'Black Five' No 5069 ready and waiting to depart for St Pancras at 8.55am. At this time an unusual working, routed via Nottingham and Melton Mowbray rather than the more usual route via Leicester.

During the short walk from the station to the workplace we may well reflect on the changes that have taken place over the last few years, and possibly anticipate in imagination those which are undoubtedly to take place over the next year or two. We can be sure more 'old favourites' are destined to follow those already departed.

Soon after settling down at work we notice the two Stockport, Heaton Mersey CLC workings arrive. They should normally have been in the care of 'D2s' Nos 4361 and 4392. Not unusually, one is absent, on this occasion No 4392, and Liverpool 'D6' No 5878 is on loan as a substitute. This is

something of a bonus for the shed, as they generally have to manage with one of their 'J10' 0-6-0s.

On the LMS side the 9.52am from St Pancras has arrived. A turn which for so long would usually produce a Bristol 'Compound', although the 'Black Fives' were becoming more frequent almost weekly. They had not yet taken over this turn completely, but on this occasion No 5097 is indeed in charge. During the morning we shall see trains arriving from Buxton, Miller's Dale and Sheffield behind Class 2 engines Nos 462, 413, 353, 400 and 487. 9.57am brings an LNER arrival from Sheffield behind 'C1' Atlantic No 4434. After turning this engine will go forward to Liverpool with a CLC fast train at 11.30am. She will then return to Sheffield via the Tiviot Dale line. 10.20am brings another 'C1' No 3299 with a train from Leicester. After she has turned she will return with the 11.22am made up of the coaches that arrived at 9.57am with the addition of through Liverpool coaches which arrive

at 11.15am. On this morning the 11.15 is brought from Liverpool behind 'D6' No 5852. As the stock from the 10.20 arrival will be required in London Road later in the day, it will be attached empty to the 12.10pm stopping train to Guide Bridge. Almost unnoticed, a second Colwick part-fitted freight has arrived at Deansgate, very late indeed; in place of the expected 'B8' on this working is 'J6' 0-6-0 No 3540. These engines were not infrequent visitors, but 'K2s' were much less common and it was a 'red letter' day if a 'J11' appeared.

During all this activity there had been a train from Chester behind a 'C13', a stopping train from Northwich behind a 'J9' and a 'J10' had arrived from St Helens. A further arrival from Chester at

Above:
LNER 'A4' Pacific No 4498 *Sir Nigel Gresley* on exhibition alongside Platform 9 in March 1938. *W. Potter*

Right:
Great Northern Stirling Single No 1 prepares to depart for Liverpool from Platform 9 on 21 September 1938. *W. Potter*

Right:
Great Northern Stirling Single No 1 prepares to depart for Liverpool from Platform 9 on 21 September 1938. *W. Potter*

Below:
Neepsend 'B17' No 2865 *Leicester City* **departing from Central on 6 May 1937.** *W. Potter*

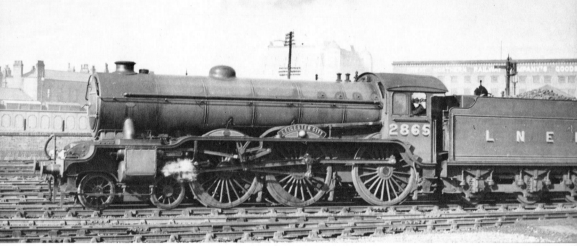

Right:
Somerset & Dorset 4-4-0 No 323, which was rebuilt by Fowler in 1921 and taken into LMS stock in 1930 is seen here at Platform 8 at Central sporting a Millhouses 19B shedplate in about 1934. *W. Potter*

0.43am, a Trafford 'C13' working, was an item of interest.

For a good many years ex-works passenger engines from Gorton were given a run out to Chester on either the 6.15 or 7.15am stopping trains, returning on the 10.43am arrival; this latter did not call at seven of the intermediate stations. The practice of running in locomotives on these trains had rather fallen into disuse by 1934; however when the 'B17s' commenced visiting Gorton works for overhaul towards the close at that year the practice was revived and so far I can trace all members of the class shopped before the outbreak of World War 2 were given a run to Chester and back, indeed very occasionally two runs. During this period I have record of very few other types appearing on this turn. On 23 April 1937 Compound Atlantic No 5364 *Lady Faringdon* had a run, as did No 5365 *Sir William Pollitt* on 7 March 1938; on 1 and 7 July 1938 the unnamed 'B4' No 6167 appeared, after fitting with Caprotti valve gear, and so did No 6166 *Earl Haig*.

Let us return to our review of the movements of 24 September 1935. At 11.16am No 6168 *Lord Stuart of Wortley* arrived with a train from Leicester Central. She would leave tender first at 12.10pm with the stopping service to Guide Bridge. On arrival at Gorton she was relieved. No 5429 *Prince Henry* working the 5.00pm run to Sheffield and returning to Central with the train from Hull in the evening. After No 5429 had returned to Gorton No 6168 again took over the diagram. Further LMS trains then arrived behind Nos 515 and 1093. There were no problems with No 1093 today and she duly set off south with the St Pancras train at 1.45pm. Apart from No 5104 already mentioned, Liverpool trains had been handled by Pollitts, Nos 5856/64/74 and 79 all being noted. Then at 12.15pm No 5855 also arrived. Following her in at 12.17pm was the other Caprotti 'B4', No 6166 *Earl Haig* with the train from Cleethorpes. Earlier in the day No 6166 had taken the 8.20am ex-London Road to Marylebone as far as Sheffield. After working the 1.08pm local to Guide Bridge there would be no respite for her. After a visit to Gorton for service she would be back at Central to work the 7.22pm up Leicester, return to Gorton and make ready for another day commencing with the 8.20am to Marylebone.

The next important departure was the 12.20pm to St Pancras, No 5097 returning as far as Derby on this train. An arrival from St Pancras 30min later was in the charge of another 'Black Five', No 5088. After a break for lunch we would be looking forward to the arrival of the Liverpool bound Boat Train. Although we would expect to find 'B17' No 2841 *Gayton Hall* coming in with the train from Ipswich as she had taken the train to Ipswich the previous day, it transpires that Ipswich's No 2807

Blickling had taken over, a fault having presumably developed on No 2841. 'D9' No 6019 is waiting to take the train on to Liverpool. A second Ipswich engine No 2820 *Clumber* arrives tender first with a Guide Bridge local at 2.29pm. She had come down the previous afternoon with the Boat Train and was now ready for her return journey. Her train duly arrives from Liverpool at 3.03pm with Neepsend Atlantic No 4420 in charge. The Atlantic had reached Liverpool with a Hull-Liverpool express running over the line from Godley Junction, through Stockport Tiviot Dale and joining the CLC main line near Glazebrook. Later in the day a further Hull-Liverpool train would travel over this same route, after which the engine would then travel to Manchester in time to work the up mail at 10.30pm. On this latter train on this day the engine would be Atlantic No 4428.

Meanwhile a second Nottingham engine, on this occasion 'Compound' No 928, had arrived with a train from London. A semi-fast from Derby is in the capable hands of '3P' 4-4-0 No 774. During the late afternoon it is noted that '4F' No 4425 is doing a stint on local passenger work, the missing 2-6-2T seems to be No 95. Also noted on Buxton and Sheffield turns are '2P' 4-4-0s Nos 546, 447 and 564. Before the evening rush-hour commenced at about 5.00pm there was a flurry of activity as No 2807 *Blickling* returned from Trafford Park to work the 4.28pm stopper to Guide Bridge, at the same time as the shed sent 'D6' No 5880 to work the 4.30pm to Liverpool.

On the LMS side a train from London arrived at 4.25pm behind No 5068. A semi-fast to Derby left behind No 928 at 4.25pm and a London train departed at 4.35pm behind No 1057; the semi-fast travelling via Tiviot Dale and Marple and being overtaken by the London train which took the shorter route via Cheadle Heath. Doncaster 'K3' 2-6-0 No 1141 arrived at Deansgate for the 5.50 York fitted goods. The next hour saw the tempo stepped up dramatically, with 32 trains being dealt with between 5.00 and 6.00pm, mostly tank engine hauled, except for a St Helens train just before 5.00pm and the 5.43 to Guide Bridge both of which were 'J10' powered. 'Black Five' No 5067 takes the 5.50pm to London and the third Nottingham engine, Compound 'No 927, brings the train from London in at 6.20pm. Other tender engine workings to be seen are the return from Guide Bridge at 5.59 of No 2807 *Blickling* (she will make her final departure at 6.28pm terminating at Fairfield) and the arrival at 6.30pm of another local from Fallowfield headed by Lincoln 'J39' No 1493. The latter will then make her way to Trafford Park sidings, very likely collecting a few wagons from the goods yard on her way. Ultimately she will depart Trafford at 7.50pm with a Class 'A' goods for

Lincoln. As we move out of the station we note that a further 'J69' No 7273 has arrived on the scene.

We must now move on about 12 months to note a rather unusual happening on the mornings of 25 and 26 September 1936, happenings which were to be repeated on the mornings of 27 and 28 April 1937. On each of these four mornings very shortly after 10.20am the LNER arrivals due at 9.57 and 10.20am arrived combined to form one train with both the rostered engines at the head. These were still Neepsend, Sheffield workings and the engines involved were 'D10' 4-4-0 No 5433 *Walter Burgh Gair* and 'C1' No 4420, and 'C1s' Nos 4420 and 4449 in 1936, and in 1937 'D11' No 5508 *Prince of Wales* and 'C1' No 4420 on both occasions. One time Gorton favourites Nos 5433 and 5508 had both moved on at last. The combined train was, in fact, of neither very great length or weight. The 9.57am consisted of a four coach lavatory set allocated to New Basford which left there at 5.18am as empty stock to Nottingham Victoria to form the 6.25am stopping train to Sheffield; there forming the 8.40am to Manchester with the addition of a lavatory composite brake, this vehicle being detached at Manchester and returning to Sheffield attached to the 10.30pm. During the summer a locked corridor third was also attached at Sheffield, to work from Manchester to Ipswich attached to the 11.22am up Barnetby and detached at Sheffield on the return working. The four coach set formed the 11.22. Also attached at Manchester and detached at Sheffield were a GE corridor brake composite running from Liverpool to Lowestoft and a GC corridor brake third running from Liverpool to Colchester. In the summer months a further corridor third was included on Friday and Saturday only, running from Liverpool to Lowestoft. After arrival at Barnetby and throughout the following two days the original four coach set made trips to Lincoln, Gainsborough (Lea Road), Sheffield, Hull, Doncaster (three times), Nottingham and Mansfield before finally arriving back in New Basford 67hr after its original departure. The 10.20am arrival was a Leicester four coach lavatory set departing from Leicester at 7.22am. After arriving in Central its next revenue earning journey was from London Road with the 3.52pm stopping train to Sheffield, from whence it then had a run to Chesterfield and back. The following day the stock made three return trips to Nottingham, followed by a single journey, finally working a stopping train to Leicester, arriving back just over 40hr after setting forth. I have recounted these details to demonstrate the diversity of LNER coaching diagrams and to illustrate the stock utilisation of the time. Conversely a further train departed from Leicester for Manchester Central at 8.02am, this consisting of four bogie corridor vehicles, plus an extra corridor third on Monday and Saturday. On arrival in Manchester at 11.16am

this set stood until 7.22pm before returning direct to Leicester.

To return to the unusual events of 1936/37, there was of course a good reason: single-line working through the down bore of the twin bore Woodhead tunnel. On the first occasion this was as a direct result of a loose-coupled goods train dividing in the up bore during the night of 24/25 September 1936. The driver continued unaware of what had occurred in the smoke filled tunnel behind him. The guard realised what had happened and managed to stop the rear portion as it was rolling backwards Before he had time to protect the rear of his train with detonators he was astonished to hear a second train approaching through the murky blackness of the tunnel. Fortunately he was able to find a refuge before the second train collided with the stationary wagons. The effect of the collision was to force a number of wagons upwards damaging the tunnel roof. During the night of 25/26 September a party of men was still working on the clearance of debris and the repair of the roof. In such cases it was regarded as inevitable that when all the damaged wagons were removed there would be some further fall of rock and debris. At about 1.45am there was such a fall, with disastrous results. The *Manchester Guardian* reported one man killed and nine injured, three sufficiently badly to be detained in Ashton-under-Lyne Infirmary. Delays to passenger trains were held at a minimum during the operations, the longest apparently being no more than 30min. I have no details of the locomotive involved. There may or may not be any significance in the presence of Gorton Class O4 2-8-0 No 6268 in the works yard shortly afterwards bearing signs of collision.

I have made exhaustive enquiries into the cause of the collision without concrete result. It seems probable that the signalman at Dunford Bridge failed to notice that the first train had no tail lamp. How far this train travelled before it was stopped is also not clear. Because there was a fatality there was an enquiry. The report does not give details of the collision, but merely confirms that a man was killed by a fall of rock whilst working inside the tunnel.

Fortunately the second incident, in 1937, was less dramatic. The up bore had to be closed owing to a rock fall. So far as I have been able to ascertain no train was involved and no person injured. As devotees will be aware, up trains approached the tunnel after a 14 mile up hill slog from Guide Bridge, and continued to climb for almost the whole of the three mile length of the bore. Goods trains were frequently put into the loop approaching the tunnel and brought to a stand. The continual pounding of the exhaust of hard working loco-motives had a very adverse effect on the tunnel roof, which was a continuing headache for the maintenance gangs. When single-line working was

Trafford Park 'N5' No 5520 on pilot duty in July 1937.

W. Potter

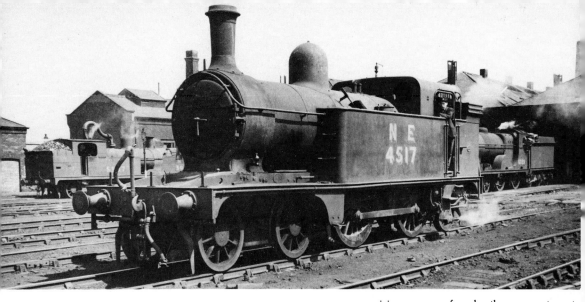

in force for maintenance purposes, usually at weekends, it was more often than not the up tunnel which was closed.

Sandwiched between the two tunnel incidents was an item of light relief at Central. On the morning of 13 February 1937, a new 'B17' 4-6-0 allocated to Gorton, No 2862, was officially named *Manchester United*. The ceremony was performed by Mrs J. W. Gibson, the wife of the club chairman, in the presence of the Lord Mayor Alderman J. Toole and other distinguished guests. I do not recall a similar ceremony when a sister engine was given the name *Manchester City*. This may have offended supporters of the latter club, they had enjoyed a far better record during the recent years including an FA Cup Final, winning the FA Cup the following year and the First Division Championship the year after. But then, they did not have their own station alongside their ground!

Moving on to 1938 I am again indebted to the *Manchester Guardian* for details of an exhibition which was held within the Central Station. This was described as an exhibition of modern rolling stock, open daily from Monday 28 February until Friday 4 March. The event was opened by the Lord Mayor Alderman Joseph Crooks Grime OBE LDD. The Lord Mayor and Lady Mayoress were then given a guided tour of the exhibition by Sir Christopher Needham, a director of the LNER. Included among the exhibits were a dining car and kitchen car of the latest design, a Tourist Stock Buffet Car, described as an LNER speciality, a Pullman car said to be 'very luxurious', a third class convertible sleeping

car comprising seven four-berth compartments convertible to day use, a camping coach comprising two sleeping compartments, living room and kitchen equipped with crockery, cutlery, linen and cooking requisites, and a Post Office mail van equipped for sorting mail and with apparatus for picking up and dropping mail without stopping the train. Finally, there was a signal demonstration van including a model railway layout embodying the latest principles of signalling and a number of working block instruments, with a team of experts on hand to give demonstrations. At the head of this train of assorted vehicles was what the younger visitors at least, and perhaps many of the not-so-young as well, considered the *pièce-de-résistance*, 'A4' 4-6-2 No 4498 *Sir Nigel Gresley*. The train appears to have spent most, if not all, of the five days alongside Platform 9. I understand that some of the faithful, unable to view the 'A4' during the week, were fortunate enough to catch 'Him' on Gorton shed the following Sunday.

As if that were not enough, September 1938 brought an even rarer treat. The preserved Great Northern 4-2-2 No 1 was on view on Monday and Tuesday 19th and 20th. On Wednesday 21 September No 1 worked a special train of period stock to Liverpool and back. This event received coverage in several newspapers. One mentioned that the train was part of celebrations to commemorate the Edinburgh Railway Races of 1888, that the journey to Liverpool took 46min, the engine being in charge of Driver D. Philpot and Fireman W. D. Short. This report included a rather indifferent picture of the train departing from Platform 9. A second report stated that the train was allowed 54min for the trip to Liverpool departing at 11.00am. 67min were allowed for the return trip. A fare of 3/2d was charged (about 16p). This report includes an excellent shot of the train at speed and asserted that 65mph was achieved at several locations.

As 1938 drew to a close, one might well have watched the comings and goings at Central and reflected upon the great changes during the decade. Only one Pollitt 'D6' remained at Trafford and six at Liverpool, three of which — Nos 5869/71/79 — are thought to have known no other shed since before the Grouping. Stockport still had their two; during the week of the exhibition in March I had noted both, Nos 5855/64, on the turns into Central. In September No 5864 had made her last journey to Gorton and had been replaced at Heaton Mersey by No 5859. She too was missing during the week of the visit of No 1, 'J10' No 5132 standing in. At this time two of the stopping trains from Northwich were noted in the charge of a 'J10' and 'N5'.

The LNER side had seen some changes among the passenger turns, although goods turns were largely as before. The two Caprotti 'B3' engines were long gone. The arrivals at 11.16am and 12.17pm were hauled by 'B17' No 2865 *Leicester City* and No 5502 *Zeebrugge* during a week in March. By September, a further reorganisation transferred these two workings to Neepsend. During the week commencing 19 September the former was in the charge of No 5437 *Prince George* and the latter was shared between Nos 5428 *City of Liverpool* and 5426 *City of Chester*. The other Neepsend turns were still largely handled by 'C1' Atlantics, except that the 10.20am arrival was usually hauled by a 'Director'. Neepsend was rapidly acquiring a large stud of 'Directors', mainly from Gorton, but also from Neasden. For about 12 months during 1937 Neepsend had 'B17s' Nos 2863/64/65. I did not have the opportunity to

speak with any of the crews to obtain their opinion of their charges. Presumably they were largely employed south of Sheffield. I only have record of one appearing on the 10.20am on nine occasions during 1937, although No 2865 did make eight consecutive appearances during January 1938, immediately before being transferred to Gorton. Also during 1937 one had charge of the 4.48pm up on a dozen occasions.

There was little change in the working of the Boat Train, except that in May 1938 Nos 2805 of Parkeston Quay and 2807 of Ipswich changed places. I cannot be absolutely certain but I do not believe No 2805 had appeared on the Boat Train prior to 1938. No 2845 seemed to have become a great favourite at Ipswich and during the period 1936-1938 the frequency of her appearances on the Boat Train far exceeded that of any other engine. Perhaps the most dramatic change took place when the 3.20pm down from London became a daily Gorton working in the spring of 1938. It is believed the change took place on Monday 3 May. Towards the end of 1938 the uninformed were no doubt startled to see the train running into Manchester behind 'A1' Pacific No 2558 *Tracery*, an event to be followed by the appearance of other Pacifics. About the same time 'V2' 2-6-2s also made their appearance. Prior to all this 22 August had brought a pleasant surprise when old favourite No 6166 *Earl Haig* had come down with the train. A Neasden engine at the time, she may well have worked right through if the rostered engine had failed in London.

Then there were the 'B7' 4-6-0s. A stud of 20 at Gorton in 1930 had been reduced only to 17 in 1935. For years these fast and powerful engines had a virtual monopoly of fitted goods trains and passenger excursion traffic, not to mention their frequent employment on ordinary passenger trains. However, by the close of 1938 their numbers at Gorton had been reduced to five, and their place

Above:
'N5' No 5520 at Central goods, in the late 1930s.
W. Potter

had largely been taken by the 'K3' 2-6-0s, although the 'J39' 0-6-0s were also often observed on fast goods trains. In postwar years it became fashionable to run down, even deride, these magnificent mixed-traffic engines. The term 'Black Pig' was used most extensively, with the inference that it had always been in common usage. I will admit to being biased in favour of the 'B7s', but must state categorically that in many hours spent on Gorton shed and in many visits to other GC sheds during the 1930s I never once heard the term used. I do not believe I ever spoke with a Great Central man who would not prefer a 'B7' to a 'K3'. As to the supposed coal-devouring capabilities of the 'B7', made so much of in postwar years, published figures show them to be about the same as similar sized mixed-traffic engines of the same period.

On the LMS the beginning of 1938 had seen the 'Compounds' largely giving way to the 'Black Fives' on the express trains. Nevertheless during the week of the exhibition Nottingham's Nos 1095 and 927 were noted (the latter three times), as was one Bristol 'Compound'. By September the 'Jubilees' had appeared on the scene, displacing some of the 'Black Fives'. During the September week no Bristol 'Compound' was seen, although No 1092 of Nottingham, No 1041 of Leicester (twice) and No 1010 of Leeds (also twice) were recorded. The appearance of Class 2P 4-4-0s on the Sheffield and Buxton trains remained fairly constant — Nos 324/32, 400/01/12/13/47/61/62/85/87, 546 and 564 all still being prominent as were Nos 323, 351 and 402. 'Crabs' were not in evidence on the Buxton turns during either week. The Millhouses turns were occasionally '4F'-worked during the week and usually so on Sundays.

The only change of significance on the local scene was on the CLC and occurred during the early part of the war when a number of Great Northern 'C12' 4-4-2Ts arrived on strength. At about the same time eight 'C13' engines were moved to Bradford. Two or three paused at Ardsley on the way, their stay being so short as to promote the thought that they had arrived there in error. One or two of the GN engines were still in the Manchester area after the war. I recall riding behind one during the winter of 1949/50. The driver was scathing in his comments, obviously preferring the 'C13s'. It would be interesting to know what was thought of the latter at Bradford. None stayed for very long, some only for weeks and the longest for less than a year.

After the war I had several runs on Midland section expresses. The previously mentioned run behind No 1000 apart, they were always behind 4-6-0s, one or two of which were quite smart. Those on the LNER, were usually behind a Thompson 'B1' (when on no occasion could I fault the locomotive), occasionally behind a 'Green Arrow' ('V2') where again I had no cause for complaint, and once behind a 'K3' from Leicester which offered a very mediocre performance in comparison with every ride I ever had on the GC section with a 'K3'.

One Sunday morning during the summer of 1947 I received a rather pleasant surprise. I patronised an excursion off the Fallowfield line to Southport Lord Street. As I waited on the platform at Wilbraham Road I expected a 'B9', perhaps with luck a 'J11', and a rake of very elderly non-corridor stock. In the event a 'B17' and buffet-car stock appeared. This was the last time that I boarded a train at Wilbraham Road. How nice to have finished in a blaze of glory!

8 Glazebrook to Godley

In my view no account of the Manchester railway scene between the wars would be complete without some reference to the Glazebrook to Godley Junction line, if only on account of Grand National Day at Aintree. Opened in four stages between 1863 and 1873, the through line was rather more than 18½ miles in length and although of a mainly rural nature could provide some interesting running.

As one left the CLC main line the track was soon climbing at 1 in 135 to clear the Manchester Ship Canal then falling at a similar gradient to Milepost 16, with an easing of the gradient through Partington station. After a short level stretch the line then began to climb again to clear the MSJ&A tracks at Timperley, rising for about 1½ miles at 1 in 150 to 1 in 420. West Timperley station was on stilts where the line crossed the Manchester-Chester road. The line then dropped steeply for ¼ mile at 1 in 74 to reach Skelton Junction near Milepost 13. At this point the LNWR line from Warrington (via Lymm) trailed in from the right and the CLC line, which connected with the MSJ&A Altrincham line and afforded access to Northwich and Chester, did so from the left. A marshalling yard and turntable were provided between the main line and the curve to the MSJ&A. The line continued to Stockport (Tiviot Dale) and was of an undulating nature with easy gradients, Tiviot Dale being at Milepost 5½. Stations were passed at Baguley, (near Milepost 12), Northenden (near Milepost 9½) and Cheadle (near Milepost 8).

Below:
Stanier '8F' 2-8-0 No 8017 eases a train of ICI hopper wagons from Peak Forest to Northwich around the sharp curve from Skelton Junction to Deansgate Junction on the MSJ&A line (not to be confused with Deansgate goods Manchester). Skelton yard and turntable are on the right. *W. Potter*

Immediately beyond the platform at Northenden a LNWR branch forked off to the right to Stockport (Edgeley), and beyond Cheadle there was a connection to the right with the Midland main line. In early days there had been a local service of sorts over the LNWR branch, but in LMS days only the odd excursion interrupted the normal pattern of goods trains. Traffic from the Midland was also largely confined to goods. The five mile stretch between Skelton Junction and Cheadle Junction could at one time boast one of the highest concentrations of goods traffic on a double track line in the country. In the Baguley area an accommodation siding was provided on either side of the line. Leaving Stockport the line climbed steeply for most of the remaining 5½ miles to Godley, much of the first two miles being at 1 in 82 with a short stretch at 1 in 63 to Bredbury Junction, the next mile to Woodley Junction continuing at 1 in 63. From this point to Apethorne Junction, a distance of rather less than ½ mile, there were running powers over Great Central & Midland Joint metals with a brief respite — the line falling at 1 in 117. The final two miles to Godley rose at 1 in 100 apart from the last few chains which were level. Trains from Godley to Stockport obviously had an easy time but there was little scope for fast running due to several severe speed restrictions.

A local service was operated between Stockport and Altrincham until 1931, with odd journeys being extended over the Great Central & Midland Joint line to Marple, and one journey on Saturdays continuing at the other end of the line to Hale. There was also a service of sorts between Stockport and Godley, contrived by extending one or two stopping trains from Liverpool or Warrington. This latter service continued throughout the interwar years, although latterly it was usually provided by a railcar. During the war however, the railcars vanished and short non corridor trains reappeared, hauled by anything between a 2-4-2T and a 'B9' 4-6-0.

Above:
Heaton Mersey shed in May 1933. The 'Flatiron' is No 2004, the '3F' in the centre will be either No 3612 or No 3638. The 'N5' is No 5928. The 'J10' is in old livery. *W. Potter*

Right:
A cold winter's day at Heaton Mersey, 2 March 1947. 'J10' No 5124 has been recently renumbered 5198, but evidently the buffer beam was overlooked.
Great Central Railway Society Collection

The enthusiasts visiting the line all had their favourite locations. I know Skelton was high on the list, and understandably so. I liked Northenden station. A delightfully somnolent spot where the seemingly endless stream of CLC goods trains hauled by the inevitable 'J10s' was occasionally interspersed with LMS or LNER goods trains with larger motive power, and even more occasionally by the railcar coming to a halt. Then suddenly, with a high pitched scream of the whistle, a GN Atlantic would tear through with a Hull-Liverpool, rousing the echoes and leaving a cloud of dust in her wake.

Quite often special and excursion trains would be routed over the line, but the day on which it really came into its own was the Friday towards the end of March when the Grand National Steeplechase was held at Aintree. On this day a number of special trains would be routed over the line such as LMS trains from the Midland and LNER trains from the GC, from Cheadle and Godley Junctions respectively. During the 1930s the number of trains was usually 17. Certain engines turned up on more than one occasion, notably Sheffield 'B7' No 5483 four times and Leicester 'Compound' No 1041 which also appeared four times. The 'star turn' was the King's Cross Pacific with her train of Pullman cars, the only occasion during the 1930s when one might expect to see Pullman Cars in the area and until the latter part of 1938 the only occasion when one might expect to see a Pacific also. It was perhaps a little disappointing that there was not as much variety as one would have liked among the Pacifics. 'A3' No 4475 *Flying Fox* was noted four times. The LNER usually had a couple of Gorton 'B7' engines standing spare at Godley Junction in case of emergencies. Many of the trains from both companies were often quite heavy and there was quite a lot of double-heading, all of which added to the interest. On the LNER side in 1931 a 10-coach load worked by No 6169 *Lord Faringdon* grew to 13 and 14 coaches in later years and the train engine was assisted by a 'D9' 4-4-0 until 1936.

Above:
A westbound coal train passing Northenden Junction behind Midland '3F' No 3200 and '4F' No 3881. Date unknown.
W. Potter

Right:
Hull Dairycoates 'O1' No 6350 which was rebuilt from an 'O4' passing through Cheadle with a class 'B' goods, August 1945.
W. Potter

Fig 13
Heaton Mersey motive power depot.

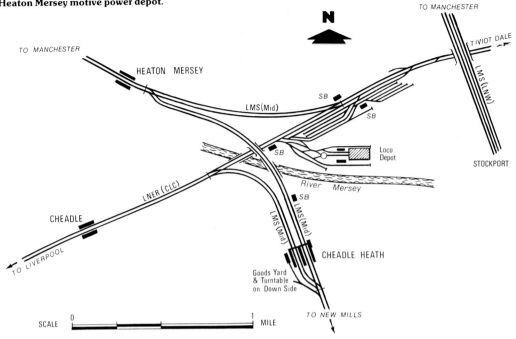

TO MANCHESTER

TIVIOT DALE

LMS(LNW)

TO MANCHESTER

HEATON MERSEY

SB

LMS(Mid)

SB

Loco
Depot

STOCKPORT

SB

River Mersey

LNER (CLC)

CHEADLE

SB

LMS(Mid)

LMS(Mid)

TO LIVERPOOL

CHEADLE HEATH

Goods Yard
& Turntable
on Down Side

TO NEW MILLS

SCALE
0 ——— 1 MILE

Subsequently the pilot was No 5424 *City of Lincoln*, assisting 'B7' No 5467 in 1937 and *Lord Faringdon* and *Valour* in 1938 and 1939 respectively. On the Midland certain trains regularly loaded to 15 coaches and 16 were noted in 1934 behind No 544 from Leicester and No 1091 from Nottingham. The usual Midland combination of Class 2 and Class 4 turned up regularly, but two 'Compounds' were also quite frequent. In 1931 Class 2 engines 430 and 437 both of Nottingham had 14 coaches. This seems rather remarkable under Midland jurisdiction, probably the load had to be increased at the last moment. Unassisted 'Compounds' with 10 coaches were observed on numerous occasions, again unusual on the Midland.

I have neither note nor recollection of any dramatic or spectacular incidents along the line during the 1920s and 1930s, neither have I unearthed any. However, Ian Allan's *Trains Illustrated* No 54 includes an interesting account by A. J. Somers describing wartime work at Heaton Mersey shed. Contained therein is a mention of a

Right:

CLC steam railcar No 600 accelerating away from Cheadle in June 1939. *W. Potter*

ather spectacular collision at Brinnington Junction between a troop train and the brake van of a goods train. The latter had been moved on to the branch out of the way of the troop train and had come to a stand with the brake van fouling the main line. The K3'-hauled troop train had taken a 'J10' as pilot for the steeply-graded line beyond Tiviot Dale, a combination which strikes me as rather incongruous.

Exhaustive enquiries and searches failed to produce any account of this in the National or Manchester papers, or in the railway press. The Manchester Library does not have any official reports for the war years. I was handicapped to some extent by the absence of a date in Mr Somers'

account. I then discovered that Heaton Mersey 'J10' No 5124 was withdrawn from traffic on 1 February 1944 and entered Gorton Works on 7 March 1944 for heavy repair after collision damage. Further searches finally revealed a short account in the *Stockport Express* of Thursday, 3 February 1944, which seems very likely to refer to this incident. The article describes a collision between a southbound express passenger train and a goods train the previous Sunday evening at a point just beyond Tiviot Dale. Six wagons and two passenger coaches were derailed. A number of passengers were shaken but were otherwise none the worse for their experience. The leading engine was completely derailed and turned on its side and

Above:
Brunswick 'J10' No 5174 with a stopping train near Cheadle in July 1938. No 5174 is believed to have spent her entire working life at Brunswick. Note the tarpaulin rolled up and fastened to the rear edge of the cab roof. *W. Potter*

Below:
Neepsend 'C1' No 4420 rushes through Cheadle with a Hull-Liverpool express in June 1939. *W. Potter*

the other was forced over to an angle of 45°. Remarkably, the only person injured was the fireman of the leading engine, Norman Street, who told the *Stockport Express*: 'I was really lucky to escape so lightly, I had just finished my stoking and had put down my shovel when there was a crash, a flash and I saw stars. The next thing I remember was as though I was awakening from a dream, my arm was being released from under the framework of the engine. My driver had been thrown clear. It was only bad luck due to the non-appearance of the fireman who should have been on duty that I was on the footplate at all'. The report went on to say that Mr Street was on the small engine which was assisting the passenger train from Stockport. The accident which occurred at 9.15pm was the first that had taken place along this stretch of the old Cheshire Lines Railway for a long time. There is no doubt in my mind this is the incident referred to in *Trains Illustrated*. Wartime regulations would probably have prevented mention of a troop train and there were no Sunday express services along the line in the normal way.

Top:
Neepsend 'B6' two-cylinder mixed traffic 4-6-0 No 5053 passing through Glazebrook with a Grand National Day special (CLC Code 13) on 24 March 1939. *W. Potter*

Above:
At the same location on the same date, another Race Special (CLC Code 16) is double-headed by 'B3' No 6165 *Valour* **(Immingham) and 'B2' No 5424** *City of Lincoln* **(Lincoln).** *W. Potter*

9 Exchange

Opened in 1884, Manchester Exchange station was immediately to the west of the Lancashire station at Victoria and lay alongside the L&Y metals. The approach roads were on a long twisting viaduct which came in behind and alongside the L&Y station at Salford and ran parallel with the latter company's tracks over the last 35 chains or so. About midway between Salford and Exchange there were connections with the L&Y in both directions. Exchange had five platforms, Nos 1 and 2 being terminal.

For myself this was never a favourite spot. If I chose to spend some time observing the traffic I preferred to be west of Eccles Junction. Here the trains came off the 'Moss' at a terrific lick. If the Eccles distant was 'on', or if the train was to stop at Eccles, it seemed that the brakes were never applied until the last possible moment. As a train entered a cutting the din competed with the overpowering aroma of iron filings. One was also well placed to observe the comings and goings along the branch curving away towards Monton Green. The bulk of traffic along this line consisted of local trains, either to Tyldesley, Atherton, Leigh and Wigan (North Western), or to Bolton (Great Moor Street). There was also a branch which left the main line at Patricroft to the west, which ran behind the engine sheds, climbed steeply to clear the Monton line and continued on to join the East Lancashire line at Molyneaux Junction. This latter branch had no passenger service but was occasionally used by excursion trains from East Lancashire to the North Wales Coast.

The sheds were situated between the main line and the Monton curve. Engine movements in and around the yard added to the varied panorama to be observed which included a sprinkling of Great Western engines, the company exercising running powers between Chester and Manchester. During the 1920s and early 1930s virtually all traffic was in

the hands of LNWR locomotive classes. Regrettably, I no longer possess any notes prior to 1931, during the summer of that year 'Precursors', 'Georges' and 'Princes' were all in full spate, with a sprinkling of 'Claughtons' on the heaviest trains. One or two of the 'Precursors' were unsuperheated, one or two 'Experiments' were in evidence as were a couple of 'Renowns', these rapidly approaching the end of their time. Among GWR locomotives noted were 'Bulldogs' Nos 3338 *Swift* and 3442 *Bullfinch*, 'Saint' No 2972 *Robin Bolitho*, and 'Halls' Nos 4934 *Hindlip Hall* and 4946 *Moseley Hall*. As time went by I visited this line rather more frequently. GWR 4-4-0s became less commonplace, although I seem to recall an afternoon turn that often produced an example, and one might occasionally turn up on pilot duties. In 1933 I noted 'Bulldog' No 3441 *Blackbird* leading 'Saint' No 2903 *Lady of Lyons* out of Exchange on one occasion. 'Halls' and Moguls became the usual order of the day, although a few 'Saints' continued to appear. During the middle and late 1930s one of the most common was No 4930 *Hagley Hall* which is now at work on the Severn Valley Railway. As the years passed the long distance cross country trains of the LMS were taken over by the large boilered 'Claughtons' and 'Baby Scots': indeed, two or three of the latter were allocated to Patricroft. Inevitably 'Black Fives' and 'Jubilees' eventually made their appearance.

In 1930 Patricroft had about 20 'Princes' on strength, three of which were withdrawn in 1934 and all except two of the remainder in 1935/36. Needless to say, they were replaced by 'Black Fives'. Likewise, the 4-6-2Ts, the tank engine version of the 'Princes', were eventually replaced by the Stanier 2-6-4Ts. At this time there were four or five unsuperheated 'Precursors' which did not last very long into the 1930s, and six superheated 'Precursors' which lasted until 1936, the last two to

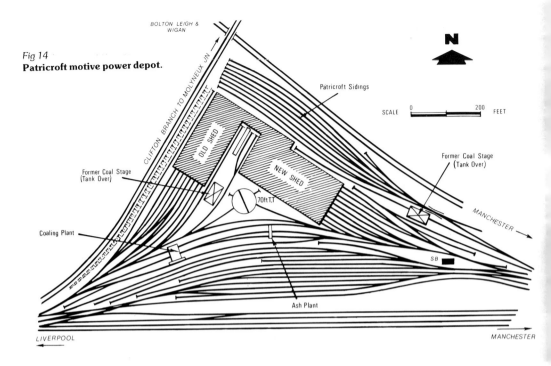

Fig 14
Patricroft motive power depot.

BOLTON LEIGH &
WIGAN

CLIFTON BRANCH TO MOLYNEUX JN.

OLD SHED

NEW SHED

Patricroft Sidings

N

SCALE 0   200 FEET

Former Coal Stage
(Tank Over)

Former Coal Stage
(Tank Over)

70ft T.T

MANCHESTER →

Coaling Plant

S B

Ash Plant

LIVERPOOL

MANCHESTER

be withdrawn being Nos 5212 *Harrowby* and 5223 *Snake* in December. A similar number of 'Georges' lasted until about the same time — No 5398, whose name had been allocated to a 'Scot', was I think the last to go in September 1936. In their later years I recall one or two of these 4-4-0s being employed on station pilot work and banking duties at Exchange. A 'Black Five' would usually be engaged upon the latter after their demise.

It has been said many times that the 'Compounds' penetrated every corner of the LMS system. On balance I would be inclined to agree, yet strangely I have no record or knowledge of any 'Compound' being allocated to Patricroft in prewar days. I cannot speak for the postwar period. That most admirable author and recorder O. S. Nock, in his fine work dealing with the 'Compounds', lists the allocations for 1933, and Patricroft does not figure therein.

During the first half of the 1930s one could always be sure of observing two or three 'Georges' from Chester or points farther west. As with the Crewe 'Princes' at London Road, there was always plenty of variety — about 20 engines in all being involved — occasionally one might also catch a 'Prince' from Llandudno Junction. 'Precursors', however (the local ones apart), were something of a rarity. One might occasionally see a 4-4-0 from Warrington, Edge Hill or Speke Junction, however, if one was a frequent visitor to London Road any such engines would probably have been observed

on numerous occasions on the MSJ&A line. Unnamed 'Princes' from Farnley Junction, Leeds were also quite regular visitors.

On a visit early in June 1932, I observed one large-boilered 'Claughton', six other 'Claughtons', three 'Princes', nine 'Georges', four 'Precursors' (including one unsuperheated), one 'Experiment', GWR Halls Nos 4937 *Langley Hall* and 4943 *Marrington Hall* and 'Saint' No 2950 *Taplow Court*. Also present of course was the usual quota of tank engines and one or two LNWR 0-8-0s. Twelve months later a similar visit produced one 'Baby Scot', one large-boilered 'Claughton', two other 'Claughtons', 10 'Princes' (including No 5816 of Springs Branch, Wigan and No 5792 of Normanton), three 'Georges', six 'Precursors' (including one unsuperheated and No 5298 *Dragon* of Crewe North, unusual but not unique) and GWR engines Nos 4970 *Sketty Hall*, 2941 *Easton Court* and 2-6-0 No 4346.

My notes indicate that one would expect to see engines from Springs Branch and Normanton in the early 1930s. Inevitably something of the glamour of the LNWR sections departed with the passing of the wonderful conglomeration of names, many of which of course had been associated with the LNWR for many years and had been borne by many locomotives. However, unbeknown to me at the time, fate still had a thrill in store and some years ahead at that. On a Saturday night in April 1947 I was on Exchange Station waiting to board the 'Irish

Left:
**Patricroft (10C) 'Precursor'
No 25211** *Aurania* **awaiting her
turn on the turntable at her home
depot, April 1936.** *W. Potter*

Below left:
'George the Fifth' No 5396
Typhon **seen rather unusually at
the head of a coal train in March
1936, about to cross from L&Y to
LNWR metals outside Exchange
station.** *W. Potter*

Mail'. I walked to the head of the train fully expecting to find a 'Black Five'. I was both amazed and delighted to be met with No 25350, once named *India*. She gave us a wonderful run. We had to wait time at Warrington and Daresbury, and Chester was also reached ahead of time, at which point the expected 'Black Five' duly took over. To digress a moment, this was not the first occasion I had been surprised by *India*. On a Bank Holiday in 1935 I had spent a rewarding day at Crewe returning on the train from Birmingham which was due at London Road at 8.05pm. I recall riding immediately behind the tender in one of those small, narrow ex-LNWR side-corridor vehicles, many of which were still to be found as late as 1939. *India* was in charge, this being I believe the only occasion prior to 1936 when I saw the train without a 'Prince' in charge.

One of the most unusual trains of stock I ever witnessed was at Patricroft on a Saturday evening excursion, when 4-6-0 No 8786 headed 19 six-wheelers and six bogies (all non corridor). I believe that to be the only occasion during the 1930s on which I saw six-wheeled LMS stock in the Manchester area, although as I have already stated it was commonplace on the LNER and on the CLC. Another unusual sight witnessed at Patricroft one evening was the arrival of a local behind a 'Black Five' running tender first. I assume the rostered tank engine had failed in Exchange. If I am not mistaken, in the early days of the Stanier engines there was a

directive that they should not run tender first on passenger trains on account of the severely restricted vision ahead afforded by the high-sided tender. Indeed it was most unusual to see any engine running tender first with a passenger train on the LNWR section, and I fancy the practice must have been frowned upon by the authorities.

Patricroft did not handle the volume of local traffic dealt with by other sheds in the area, but they did have a stud of LNWR 4-6-2Ts for many years, which were eventually replaced by Stanier's 2-6-4Ts. For many years the local traffic along the Monton line was handled by the LNWR 0-6-2 Coal Tanks, most of which were shedded at Plodder Lane. In particular Nos 7692, 7703/15/22/56 and 69 figure prominently in my records. There was also a turn into and out of Exchange during the evening which was usually worked by the ex-Wirral Railway Aspinall 2-4-2T No 6762 from Springs Branch shed. If she was absent for any reason the substitute would be another member of the class — usually No 10639 or No 10641 I think. No 6762 was in fact originally L&Y No 1041. Sold to the Wirral Railway in 1921, she had been allocated the number 10638 thus taking her place among the L&Y engines. How or why she came to be numbered 6762 is not clear. She lasted well into BR days.

The Monton line curved away very sharply and was well cambered. My strongest memory is of the diminutive Coal Tanks heeling over sharply as they rattled around the curve with steam off and the

'Prince of Wales' 4-6-0 No 25683 *Falaba* (Chester 6A) slipping away to Patricroft in June 1937. One of the four 'Princes' which survived to BR days, she was at Camden during the early 1930s when something of a rarity in Manchester. *W. Potter*

'tinny' feeble sounding exhaust when the regulator was opened on leaving the curve. The Newton Heath or Polmadie 'Baby Scots' drifting around with the Glasgow trains left a much fainter impression. Occasionally one would be treated to the sight (and sound) of an LNWR 0-8-0 struggling valiantly to surmount the steep incline behind the sheds which led on to the East Lancs line.

There were one or two mishaps in and around Manchester Exchange. On 1 May 1928 two goods trains collided where the lines converged near Stalybridge. A total of 14 wagons were derailed and a further 20 damaged. One engine was damaged, but fortunately there were no injuries. The accident occurred at about 3.40am blocking both Standedge lines and resulting in the destruction of some 40yd of track. Traffic resumed at 8.30am with diversions and some delay. After good work by the repair gang it was possible to resume normal working by 11.00am.

Owing to thick fog on 22 January 1929, a Liverpool-Newcastle express had slowed down to a crawl approaching Manchester. A few hundred yards short of Exchange Station it collided with an empty stock train which was stationary at the time. Two of the empty coaches left the rails but did not turn over. Guard Edward Rose of Oldham and a brakman were thrown to the ground, the brakeman suffering an injury to his eye. Passengers were unaware that there had been a collision and none complained of injury or shock. Several yards of track were damaged. The train, due into Newcastle at 2.20pm, did not get away from Manchester until 11.00am, 1½hr after the collision.

In the early hours of 19 October 1931 the 12.50am Manchester Exchange-Leeds newspaper train collided with the 10.00pm Liverpool-Miles Platting goods near Collyhurst Street signalbox at Miles Platting. All lines were blocked by the derailment of a locomotive and 10 wagons. Leeds received the newspapers 3hr late that morning.

On 9 August 1932, through carriages were being moved for attachment to a train for Carlisle and Scotland. During the operation a collision occurred with a goods train. The passenger engine was damaged, 12 wagons were derailed and there was some track damage. No passengers were injured and there was no damage to the coaching stock but the departure of the Carlisle train was delayed.

At Eccles Junction on 5 September 1936 a light engine left the rails and crashed into the signalbox. There was considerable damage to the cabin but fortunately no injuries. On 20 January 1938 a Leeds-Liverpool express running down Miles Platting bank had one coach slightly damaged when it came into contact with one of six wagons which had derailed on the adjacent track.

The disaster which happened at Eccles at 8.18am on 30 December 1941 involved the 6.53am Kenyon Junction-Manchester Exchange and the 6.53am Rochdale-Pennington. The leading roles were played by Signalman Lowe in Eccles signalbox and Driver F. Mountfield and Fireman R. Ashcroft working the Pennington-bound train with 'Prince' tank No 2406. The Manchester-bound train was behind Stanier 2-6-2T No 207. In common with a number of accidents, this incident is of interest on account of the number of unfortunate circumstances which accumulated until the stage was set for catastrophe. In the first instance, owing to the war which was in progress, 'Summer Time' was in force and although it was December it was therefore still dark at 8.18am. To add to this there was thick fog, indeed there had been such fog about all the previous day and night and services were seriously delayed. Then there were the three fogmen with rather similar sounding names: Patton, Pantling and Parrington. Signalman Lowe appears to have become a little confused regarding these men and their whereabouts. In fact one of them had not yet arrived on duty. His previous shift not having ended until 11.30pm the previous evening, he was not therefore required to resume duty until 8.30am. It has been suggested on Lowe's behalf that he was new in the box and not conversant with the three fogmen, but I understand that he had been at the box for several weeks and in fact had only moved down from Eccles Junction, no more than ½ mile away. The running of the two trains also had some bearing on events — No 207 had dropped 49min on reaching Eccles and No 2406 had lost 27min.

Hard on the heels of No 207 was a further train which had come in behind off the Monton line. Lowe decided to put No 207 and her train across from the slow line to the fast out of the way of the Monton line train. Meanwhile No 2406 was approaching with her train along the down slow line, to reach the fast line No 207 would have to cross the path of No 2406. Lowe of course realised this, but under the impression that a fogman was already in position at his own distant he accepted 2406 intending to hold her at his home signal. In the event there was nobody to place a detonator in position at the distant signal and it would seem that neither Mountfield nor Ashcroft observed the signal. Mountfield said he had left it to the fireman as it was on his side; Ashcroft for his part said he saw the distant and it was showing green. No 2406 arrived at the crossover at the Manchester end of Eccles station just in time to cut the up train in two.

Maj G. R. S. Wilson conducted the enquiry and concluded that Driver Mountfield and to a lesser degree Fireman Ashcroft were largely to blame, having failed to maintain a proper look-out and having travelled too fast in the prevailing weather conditions. Ashcroft was not a passed fireman despite having 17 years firing experience. Maj

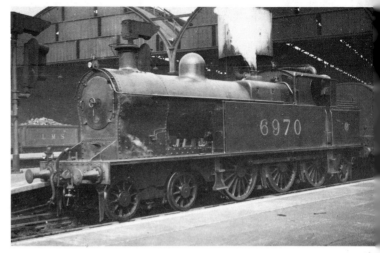

Right:
Patricroft-based Bowen Cooke 4-6-2T No 6970 about to move empty stock at Exchange in May 1935. Note the old-style livery. Edge Hill (8A) large boilered Caprotti 'Claughton' No 6029 is just visible at Platform 3.
W. Potter

Wilson obviously thought Ashcroft an unreliable witness and was unable to accept his testimony. He further thought that some portion of the blame had to be attributed to Signalman Lowe.

Then there are the 'ifs'. If it had not still been dark, if it had not been foggy, if one train had not been 49min late and the other 27min late, if Signalman Lowe had exercised a little more thought regarding the disposition of his fogmen, if the train off the Monton line had been a few minutes earlier or later, if Mountfield and Ashcroft had exercised a little more care. Consider any one of those 'ifs' and the tragedy might never have taken place.

Mention must be made of a rather remarkable journey I once made to Leeds. At one time during the 1930s, one could purchase on Sundays a half-day excursion ticket for Leeds and travel by a normal Liverpool-Leeds service train. At one time the train engine was usually a large boilered 'Claughton' and one or two of us quite often made the trip, if only to add to our experience of LNWR types at a time when opportunities to do so were becoming increasingly rare. On one Sunday morning the train arrived in Manchester rather late behind a 'Black Five'. I asked the guard if there had been some hold up on the way and he replied with something to the effect that they had stopped at St Helens Junction and that for some reason there had been considerable difficulty in getting the engine to restart. After we had boarded, the train eventually moved off with the banker working furiously in the rear and we were put across to take the left hand curve at the East end of Victoria on to the Thorp's Bridge line. We then proceeded to a point nearly adjacent to Newton Heath Sheds, where we pulled up and an old Midland '4F' 0-6-0

Below:
Ex-Wirral Aspinall 2-4-2T No 6762 (Springs Branch 10A) ready to depart for the Monton line, May 1935.
W. Potter

Above:
The first of the 'Baby Scots' No 5500 *Croxteth* (Camden 1B) ready to leave Platform 3 in May 1936. *W. Potter*

Below:
Patricroft Whale 19in 4-6-0 No 8815 with original pattern boiler on pilot duty at Exchange in May 1938. Radial tank No 10641 is in the background. *W. Potter*

No 3968, was attached to the rear of the train. The journey was then resumed in the reverse direction around the curve to Miles Platting and a further stop. After some little time the train again set off and, to my astonishment, proceeded to run all the way to Leeds with the engine running tender first. With the low Midland tender I imagine it must have been an exceedingly draughty ride for the footplatemen! I have often wondered why No 3968 was not turned on the triangle at Miles Platting. It so happened that the stock had obviously been used on the 'Sunny South Express' the previous day and the headboards had not been removed. As we drew into Stalybridge, by this time about an hour late, these headboards drew some very adverse comment from the waiting passengers along the platform!

If one travelled towards Manchester, one might observe, shortly after passing Eccles, a turnout into sidings on the left and two tracks running parallel with the main line for several hundred yards down a falling gradient. Eventually these tracks veered away to the right, burrowed beneath the main line, went around a severe and steeply cambered curve, passed several sidings and continued on to connect with the Manchester Ship Canal Co system on the docks. If one was fortunate one might observe an LNWR 0-8-2T drifting down the gradient and grinding around the curve with her train, or alternatively struggling back up the bank, enshrouded by steam and accompanied by the usual strange cacophony of wailing sounds which so often marked the progress of LNWR engines.

Wartime workings featured increasing numbers of Stanier locomotives. In particular Patricroft's allocation of 'Black Fives' increased along with the number of tank engines including six 2-6-2Ts. Two or three 'Jubilees' also turned up to displace the 'Baby Scots'. LNWR passenger engines were rather thin on the ground by this time and only occasionally might one be found in Manchester. Patricroft's three 19in mixed-traffic 4-4-0s continued to figure prominently for a year or two on station pilot and empty stock workings as well as on pick up goods turns. Needless to say the 'G2' 0-8-0 goods engines ('Fat Nancies') were still well to the fore and the 0-8-2Ts continued to wend their way up and down to the docks. The Plodder Lane Coal Tanks lasted out for some years and indeed on one occasion a friend booked No 7703 showing a Preston plate, just what she was doing in Manchester is not clear, she may possibly have been on loan to either Plodder Lane or Patricroft.

The Farnley Junction (Leeds) turns had already gone over to 'Jubilees' prior to the war, and the same batch No 5703-5706 continued for a number of years. One of the most striking changes would seem to have been the steady turn out of

Top:
Top:
Bowen Cooke '6F' 0-8-0 No 9213, having come down Miles Platting Bank and through Victoria, is crossing over to LNWR metals in June 1937. *W. Potter*

Above:
Rebuilt 0-8-0 No 8905 at Patricroft in August 1935. She was a sister engine of the unfortunate No 8903 which ran away down Miles Platting Bank in December 1947. *W. Potter*

'Compounds' on the North Wales jobs, which continued to the end of LMS days. They appear, as usual, to have performed in an excellent manner, often with loads which would have raised a few eyebrows at Derby in earlier years. I am advised that with the commencement of hostilities an early reduction of the number of GWR workings became apparent and that they eventually ceased entirely. Nevertheless a friend managed to record in the early days six each of Moguls and 'Halls' of which only 2-6-0 No 6362 and No 5909 *Newton Hall* had been regular visitors in my earlier days at Eccles Junction.